Design
and
Technology
5–12

Design
and
Technology
5–12

PAT WILLIAMS and DAVID JINKS

 The Falmer Press

A member of the Taylor & Francis Group
London and Philadelphia

UK   *The Falmer Press, Falmer House, Barcombe,*
      Lewes, East Sussex, BN8 5DL

USA   *The Falmer Press, Taylor & Francis Inc.,*
      242 Cherry Street, Philadelphia, PA 19106-1906

First published in 1985
Cover design by Trixie Selwyn
Design by Sue Ryall
Printed in Hong Kong by Imago Publishing Ltd

Reprinted 1989 (Twice)

Contents

Glossary of Terms

PVA Adhesive: an inexpensive water soluble adhesive used in the majority of primary schools.

Alloy: a mixture of two or more metals — brass is an alloy of copper and zinc.

Ampere: the unit by which an electric current is measured.

Catalyst: a substance used to speed up a chemical change in another substance.

Compression: to force into a smaller space.

Concrete-Aggregate: any material mixed with cement to form concrete.

Concrete-Retarders: a substance added to a concrete mix to slow down the setting or curing time.

Coping Saw: a tool used to cut curved/circular shapes in wood.

Cored solder: an alloy of tin and lead with a low melting point. The core of the solder is a resin, acting as a flux in helping the solder to flow around the joint.

Design: to prescribe some form, structure, pattern or arrangement for a proposed thing, system or event. *Keitn-Lucas Report 1980*

Designing: the process of seeking a match between a set of requirements and a way of meeting them or finding an acceptable compromise. *Keitn-Lucas Report 1980*

Handicraft: a collective term that was applied in secondary schools to woodwork, metal work and technical drawing.

Jig: a device used to hold or support materials during practical operations.

OHM: the unit by which electrical resistance is measured.

Reed switches: an electronic switch activated by a magnet.

Tactile: the sense of touch.

Technological awareness: having an understanding of technology and its possible effects on society.

Technology: the application of scientific, material and human resources to the solution of human needs.

Volt: the unit by which electromotive force is measured.

**Dedicated to
Bill & Margaret**

We should like to acknowledge the help given by teachers and children in schools in Berkshire, Doncaster and Rotherham.

1 So Now It's Design Technology

The activities of designing and making should be regarded as being, at the fundamental stage, every bit as important as reading, writing and arithmetic, and at the more advanced stages, as important as literature, science and history. Every child in every school, every year should be involved in designing and making activity, on the grounds that, in its own right, it is a very valuable educational approach.

(Extract from the Stanley Lecture: *A Coherent Set of Decisions* — Sir Alex Smith, Royal Society of Arts, London, 22 October 1980)

It seemed a very ordinary red car, the tissue box body with its wobbly wheels and the length of string tied to a piece of wood, to be pulled along the ground no doubt. For the two six-year old boys who made it, it was a success. Success? Why? Was it meant to do something in particular? Their two days work had been a journey of exploration and excitement, frustration and achievement, because the ordinary red car represented the solution to a very precise design brief: to make an object which would travel across a table top and stop at the edge. The red car now assumes a quite different significance, not just the naively pleasing work of a young child, but a sophisticated, precise and appropriate response to a clearly identified problem. So much is there: the shared experience of failure and reconsideration, because cardboard wheels not centred correctly won't travel and you do need an axle; the choice of an appropriate material — the tissue box was light and ready made; a genuine understanding of the mathematical relationship between the length of the string and the height of the table, a basic appreciation of the notion of force, the quick decision making and the wealth of linguistic opportunities. The children were in no doubt as to the quality of the experience — It was good.

> The Piece of string must be as long as the table is high. When the wood reaches the floor it stops the cart.

Experimenting with the little red car.

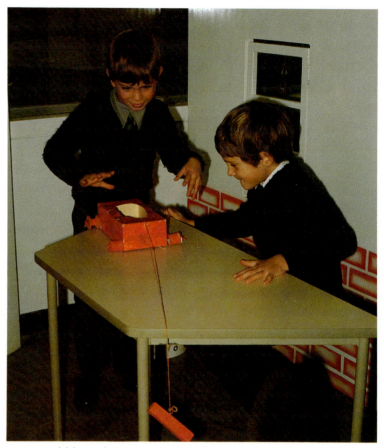

It would have been so easy to discount the value of what had taken place and yet it was so very real and relevant. It is this reality and relevance which establish the place for design technology in the primary curriculum.

Primary education is constantly being challenged to achieve a further degree of 'realism' through the experiences it offers children: the 'feeling' for mathematics identified by Cockcroft, writing for an identified audience, enjoyment as a respectable criteria for learning to read. This realism is essential in a world which is rapidly changing as it identifies a kind of learning which will have a lasting relevance. If this 'realism' is essential it must also be appropriate — and it is the appropriate design technology experience which has so much to offer the individual and society.

Design Technology is about designing and communicating, making, testing and evaluating, encouraging children to go beyond their first ideas and seek alternatives so that they may more effectively influence and control the environment in which they live. In the primary school children will naturally tend to an

investigative style of learning; their inventive urge is not inhibited by pre-conceived notions of what is acceptable and the desire to communicate is very strong and urgent. They are anxious to handle materials and to question processes. They are, in fact, beginning to develop a technological awareness. Yet our attention is repeatedly drawn to the very limited opportunities which exist.

In the 1978 Primary Survey, attention was focussed on the limited materials in use in the primary schools and the lack of development of skills in handling them. This concern was echoed in the 5–9 Survey (1982). Similarly, both surveys identified little three-dimensional work.

The Littlewick Licker — put a stamp on the tongue, turn the ears to wind on the tongue. Pour water in the top — it travels down a tube to the back of the tongue. Wind out the tongue.

The comparative neglect of three dimensional construction is disappointing: opportunities should be provided for the older children, both boys and girls, to undertake some work with wood and other resistant materials and to learn to handle the tools and techniques associated with them.

5.95 *Primary Education in England* (1978)

The number of classes involved in three-dimensional work was comparatively small and a limited range of materials was used.

2.143 *Education 5–9* (1982)

Both surveys urged the need for children to learn skills in context and they gave high priority to the development of problem solving and thinking skills. Even within the opportunities which do exist, it is often possible for the activity to be presented in such a way that its appeal is more immediately to boys than girls and play activities all too frequently reinforce sex-stereotypes.

At the national level concerns of a similar nature exist. This country, which gave birth to the Industrial Revolution and led the world of manufacturing industry, is now a net importer of manufactured goods. The ideas are there but the Department of Industry recently found it necessary to mount an exhibition, 'Designed in Britain, Made Abroad'; what is lacking is the commitment to making. Applications to study applied sciences fail to show any significant increase. At the present time the proportion of women engineers is something under 1 per cent, far less than other European countries. Attitudes are formed early but change slowly and with difficulty. It is too late at secondary level to try to counter the vagaries of the educational system and to reverse social pressures, but perhaps it is possible at primary level to change the emphasis so that 'making' is accorded some status and the teaching opportunities provided by practical problem solving fully appreciated. This is not to suggest that the role of Design Technology is simply to promote 'education for capability', of equal concern is the social and cultural dimension it brings to the whole curriculum.

CDT helps to develop in people such qualities as imagination, inventiveness, resourcefulness and flexibility. Industry and commerce need people with such qualities, but people as individuals also need these qualities in order that they may be able to challenge and change their own roles in life if they so wish. — *Equal Opportunities in CDT.*

If Design Technology is to develop within the primary curriculum then it undoubtedly presents a challenge, but it is a challenge and not a revolution. It involves looking at what is already happening and putting it together rather differently. A different emphasis will be necessary, particularly an acceptance that even the most basic of basic skills are best and most readily learned within a relevant context. As David and Steven tried to find a piece of wood to pull their car across the table, appropriate vocabulary developed: too big and too small were rapidly discarded in favour of heavier and lighter as the distinction between size and weight was clarified. As leadership changed sides, styles of language altered. The teacher was aware of the opportunities offered by the·design brief but, in one sense, could not control them since she could not predict the children's response. Her skill lay in appreciating the children's need to handle and collect apparently rather aimlessly — until the right piece of wood emerged; their need to find a book which showed how wheels went on a car, and when physical skills were not adequate, their need for assistance in fixing the wheels. In all this activity the use of time is critical. Once challenged, the child needs to complete his task. To break for a 'phonic group' or to read to Mrs. Jones perhaps says something about the teacher's perception of the value of the task.

A similar point was made in the 5–9 Survey:

While the children were drawing, painting or modelling, the teacher was busy helping children with work in the base skills. Thus the educational value of art and craft was often not realised.

The challenge exists too in terms of classroom organization and the availability of resources. But the challenge is in essence no different to that of organizing for practical experience in mathematics or science or working in groups for other activities. What is essential is that the child has access to a variety of materials — wood, plastic, metal — and also the appropriate tools. The appropriate plastic for the seven-year old may be the washing-up

A roundabout made by infant children

liquid bottle, but is he encouraged to identify and appreciate its particular qualities and so learn to discriminate and choose the most appropriate material?

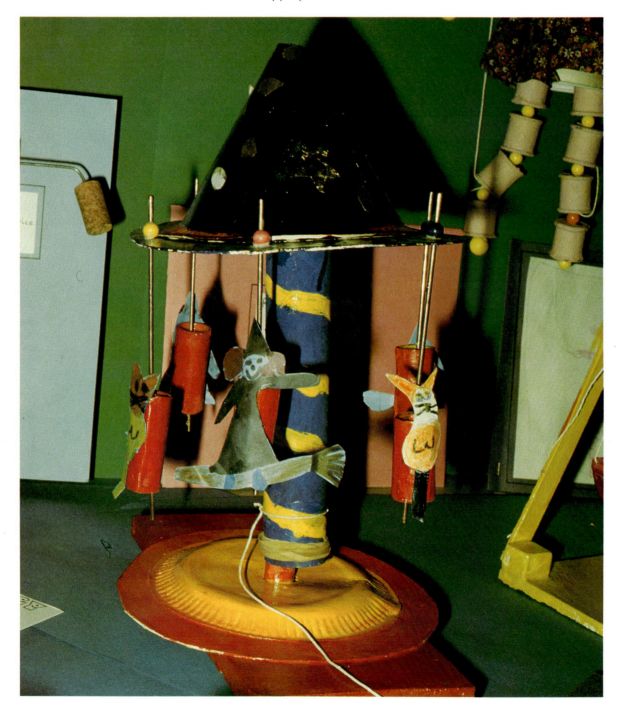

Outside the classroom an even greater challenge exists in developing the role design technology has to play in the primary curriculum. It can clearly link and give meaning and relevance to many subject disciplines. Perhaps more important is the shift in values and attitudes it can encourage away from only the academic to an appreciation of social and problem solving skills. Design Technology offers a natural group activity — not the maths group busily occupied, each on the same page, but working individually — an opportunity to ask other people for help in a most acceptable way and to respond to and modify their suggestions in an attempt to provide an acceptable solution. In classrooms where so many 'open-ended' activities are in fact so tightly fenced, Design Technology offers the child a real opportunity to make decisions and to quickly appreciate feedback both in terms of the solution and of its effect on the group.

Looking for improvements — the decision must be made together.

And what of the teacher as the child delightedly explores the real world that he can actually influence? Uncertainty? Hesitation? Perhaps inevitably this is so. Most teachers would very confidently rank pieces of written work according to the chronological age of the child. How? By a series of professional judgements built up not just by themselves but by all the teachers who have gone before. If pressed to explain the ranking they will refer, for example, to presentation, content, sentence construction, and yet none of these criteria were expressed before the selection. In Design Technology no such body of professional judgements exists. It will take time to develop a register of what is appropriate and perhaps we shall be surprised by the ability we encounter — like the seven-year-old boy who had constructed a series of interlocking wheels and could quite confidently predict the direction the speed in relative terms of any further wheel to be added — an understanding of the concepts of gearing, ratio, drive — perhaps not quantified but quite clearly there. Technological development is taking place in the normal curriculum but how well do we appreciate the level of understanding that primary children really have? How many more red cars could we see?

DISCUSSION POINTS

1   What 'making' activities exist within your school?
2   Do these activities show a development as the children progress through the school in terms of materials; and skills?

What does a lessin look like? Sounds small and slimy. They keep them in glassrooms. Whole rooms made out of glass. Imagine.

Roger McGough

2 Design Technology — Is it Appropriate at Primary Level?

Craft Design Technology is developing in the secondary schools from the traditional practices of handicraft. It has a very distinctive philosophy — developing intellectual capacity and practical skills through designing and making. Craft Design Technology — a rather trendy title — and at first perhaps not appropriate for primary school, and yet it is through Design Technology which is very much in tune with the primary school ethos, that primary education can make a very relevant curriculum response to the 1980s.

If Design Technology is to develop in the primary school it must be seen to have a primary identity, one which will arise from the strengths and needs of the primary phase. Design Technology shares with the philosophy of primary education a commitment to three concepts: first hand experience, integration and process. Children of primary age are still in the business of collecting experiences which they are gradually learning to sift and order and between which to discriminate. The primary classroom strives to provide concrete first hand experiences and yet in a way these may be said to be contrived, at one step from reality. Design Technology cannot take place without an involvement with materials and this involvement is necessary and real. For the primary child knowledge is still largely a whole, subject disciplines are only gradually beginning to emerge, and discreet concepts still being formed. To solve a design problem work will stretch across the curriculum from planning skills, precise measurement, re-search skills to formal descriptive writing on craft work, each being brought into play as it becomes necessary. The need is identified by the child who quite clearly understands the purpose of the task he is engaged upon. And what of the process? Design Technology has no specific factual content although it is possible to identify a range of concepts, skills and attitudes appropriate to the process. It is essentially concerned with a four part process of

1 Identification of need or problem
2 Proposal of solutions
3 Realizing the design: making
4 Evaluation/testing.

This process is about learning to learn, acquiring information because there is a need to know and appreciating quickly and accurately the success or failure of your own decisions.

If Craft Design Technology developed at secondary level there is no need for it to exist in the primary phase purely at a watered down level. It will be different in the same way that mathematics may be coloured buttons in sets at five years and a formal statement of logic at sixteen. Each activity has its own validity. At primary level the role of Design Technology is particularly to develop a technological awareness and to begin to build an understanding and capability; an understanding and acceptance that problems do not have a single solution and that we are able to respond to our environment in many ways and at many levels. The future quality of our man made environment is our responsibility.

This identity will take time to develop as a body of professional judgements is slowly accumulated and we are more accurately able to assess the suitability of design briefs, tools and materials for use in the primary classroom. Whilst we do not know what children may achieve in this process, we can say with some certainty that many good beginnings are lost. Infant children with constructional materials are developing and experimenting with a range of mechanical and scientific concepts. Too often the appropriate questions which will extend the child's thinking and define the concept more clearly are not asked. A group of infant children constructing a merry-go-round and using an old record player turntable had difficulty getting the balance of the bases equal with the result that the wheel turned with a rather drunken abandon. 'How can we make sure that all the bases weigh the same?' The result was a demand for 'proper scales' and an introduction to the use of a standard unit.

In essence, Design Technology already exists within the primary curriculum. Making and doing have for a long time played an important part in primary education, from the beautifully worked samplers of the Victorian era through binca and felt to the wide

The crane moves in various directions. Under the plate are table tennis balls acting as ball bearings and allowing the crane to rotate freely.

The crane, made by 9-year-olds, lifted a child in a classroom chair.

range of techniques now apparent in many primary schools. These activities are not often seen as part of a process and are very seldom used to create in three dimensions or to produce a working model. Many problems arise in the storage of three-dimensional work in the normal busy classroom — perhaps this is why children respond with such enthusiasm to handling resistant materials and enjoy the solidity and permanence of their creation. In the infant classroom the need to handle is fully accepted but even before children leave primary school the 'hands off' syndrome is developing and yet to fully appreciate the potential and quality of the material, handling may be essential and for the child an essential part of his emotional and aesthetic development.

Even adults given a practical problem will need to handle and feel the materials they will use. Do we really want children just to look with their eyes?

There is a direct relevance for the primary school in the kind of learning which Design Technology encourages. 'It is an action based approach to learning and to the context in which the subject matter appears.' (*Design in the Middle Years*) It starts where the child is at, enabling them to take account of the very sophisticated world in which they operate — even infant children will use a video and microwave with ease and approach a computer with confidence. Its relevance is not restricted to the immediate experience, in choosing a material it is not just colour and shape but how the material behaves, seeing common factors which lead to generalization and the ability to discriminate — a necessary ability in a material dominated society.

The process provides a context for the learning of a variety of skills, communication, practical, reasoning and interpersonal skills. The child who measures the playground must get little satisfaction from knowing it is x metres long, particularly if a metre is still a rather vague notion. Is x metres right — is that good or bad? It might be more interesting if he measures it to see if it is larger than another playground at the next school. Often, however, the activity remains isolated — the information unused. These children measuring are in no such doubt — their accuracy is essential, their own planning requires that and the measurement is actually used.

A group of headteachers involved in a similar practical problem-solving session exhibited every kind of group interaction and were clearly aware of the unavoidable requirements of the group — to contribute, to lead, to persuade, to assist — and this was quite apart from the actual physical construction which took place. We have such high expectations of ourselves as teachers to provide opportunities for social learning and yet these are often very difficult to create without the children feeling it is a 'fix'. Genuine group activity of this kind allows children to exhibit a range of behaviours which are often difficult to accommodate in other activities — even the non-academic may well have leadership potential!

Design Technology is nothing if not child-centred in the best possible sense, starting as it does from the child's own experience and allowing them, through the design process, to absorb feedback at their own level. Since the child has been involved in the formulation of the problem and chosen the strategies for its

Primary headteachers exploring materials and constructional techniques

solution, he is able to take part in the evaluation. Throughout the process he has been involved in decision-making at each stage: he feels that this is his activity, under his direction. This involvement produces a high level of motivation and perhaps we should now consider the way in which the methodology of design technology will affect the primary curriculum.

DISCUSSION POINTS

1   In what ways do you provide opportunities for children to:
>   plan
>   evaluate
>   use problem solving skills?

2   What use is made of three-dimensional displays within your school? Are these simply decorative? Are children encouraged to touch and handle objects?

3   In what ways in your school do you draw attention to the particular properties of materials?

Teachers need to be clear not only about what they would like children to become under their guidance, but about what children are actually like when the process is begun.

Margaret Donaldson *Children's Minds*

3 Where Do You Put Design Technology in the Primary Curriculum?

The 1960s and 1970s have seen a vast number of curriculum projects. Each successive report which has been published has indicated yet another aspect of the curriculum which deserves and requires further attention, so much so that teachers may well cry: 'Enough. Where do we fit in anything else — does design technology not further increase the clutter of the curriculum?' Perhaps comfort may be found in the suggestion that Design Technology is not 'as well as' but 'instead of' of because of the particular role it has to play.

Design Technology is not a process which lends itself to fragmentation in terms of time — an hour today — perhaps some time tomorrow. Involved in the detective work of a search for a solution the child needs to follow the leads before they grow cold — to try the idea, to find the picture, to make the wheel. During this time, maths, reading, recording of experience will take place, perhaps not in the guise in which they so often appear — the 'reading book', the maths workcard — but nevertheless, what is being offered is genuine mathematical and language experience which is of equal if not greater value than the rather more isolated practice of skills.

Its first role is to create a context within which real opportunities will arise for children to acquire and practise a range of skills. The starting point may be a deliberately constructed design brief or may arise from work already under way in the classroom. The teacher will be aware of the potential of each stage in the design process and will feed in ideas and materials where necessary but it will be the children who will identify the skills they need to develop or acquire because they perceive them to be necessary and appropriate. The children, using a right angled piece of card to reinforce a structure, quickly found a way of constructing accurate right angled triangles by drawing a square and cutting across the diagonal. The discussion took a few minutes: 'Squares have got right angles.' 'If we draw that diagonal, are both parts the same?' 'Is it better than just sticking the wood together?' 'Yes, look how the shape holds the pieces together', and so on. David and Steven making the little red car needed to look at model cars and Lego as well as lots of pictures before they could fit an axle to their box. The experience is real in the sense that weighing little boxes is not and it is this reality which we think children find so highly motivating. The experiences they have collected are fitted together as the design is realised. Science, maths, art and language came naturally together as they do in normal experience outside the world of school. It is the ability to use skills and knowledge in a variety of situations that is the true test of understanding.

Design Technology may also play a role in facilitating the integration of subjects. We are fortunate that the flexibility of most primary schools will allow children to learn in the way most appropriate to their level of development. Some ten and eleven-year-olds in project work are still at the stage of collecting and sorting experience whilst others are quite clearly anxious to discriminate between kinds of knowledge and will begin to appreciate the historical nature of history, the geographical nature of geography, etc. It is not always necessary or desirable that every project should cover every discipline — although for some in the 1960s this was what project meant! Using the design process offers the opportunity to take from each subject area what is necessary at that time and to use that information in conjunction with information from other areas, highlighting the child's perception of the nature of knowledge.

There is also an important development role for Design Technology to play in developing the child's spatial awareness and enabling and encouraging them to make some kind of visual response to their environment. It is interesting to note that the Girls into Science and Technology (GIST) Project found during tests of eleven-year-olds that girls achieved poorer results in tests of spatial ability than boys. They suggest that this may be directly related to concrete experiences which girls either lack or do not choose. The project goes on to suggest that performance in spatial ability tests may be improved by learning experiences in CDT.

If schools develop a primary identity for Design Technology, will what happens be different from present practice? What will happen will be that learning activity will take place in a total context and that the design process as a way of learning will be explicitly stated. It has already been said that at least one stage — that of making — is already well established in the primary school, albeit with limited materials and tools and not always an identifiable development of skills. It is the planning and evaluation in particular which will become more explicit and it is precisely these skills which have already been identified as so essential in much of the work done on science in recent years. It is the ability to think clearly and logically, to analyze, to determine relevance, to discriminate, identify useful information, make generalizations, form hypotheses for testing and exercise judgement that will be developed.

> **Insufficient attention was given to ensuring proper coverage of key scientific notions; the teaching of processes and skills such as observing, the formulating of hypotheses, experimenting and recording was often superficial.**
>
> 5.66 *Primary Education in England* (1978).

For thinking skills, as with social skills, it is often difficult to create situations where we are sure children will have an opportunity to acquire and use certain skills. We may set up group discussions and consider particular situations with the class when Jimmy taunted beyond his endurance, finally lashes out use logic problems, all of which have their place, but it is in activities which approximate closest to the real world that these skills develop most naturally and easily.

A place may also be created for a new emphasis on drawing as an acceptable means of recording and communicating. There must be many children who have difficulty in expressing themselves in writing but who can sketch and draw in fine detail. Deliberately requiring a two-dimensional response suggests to the children that this is an acceptable way in which they can express themselves and one in which it is often possible to convey a great deal of detailed information. Gary used his drawings to explain how his rocket base would work — the perspective may be confused but the graphics have intent.

Much has been done to prepare the way for Design Technology. The attention given to science over the last decade has helped to heighten and develop the primary teachers awareness of the need for children to develop an investigative approach to learning, to formulate hypotheses and to consider the notion of a

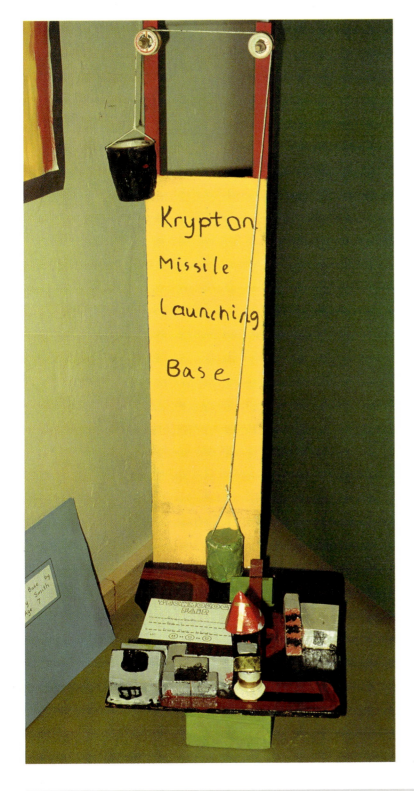

Krypton

Missile

Launching

Base

A falling weight launches the rocket.

fair test. Cockcroft has again restated the need for practical experiences and learning in context. The design process has much in common with these approaches which have already been the basis of much in-service work. The media too have developed programmes aimed at awakening technological capability and problem-solving skills at primary level: 'Ideas in Action', 'The Bicycle Programme', etc. Industrial Training Boards and Schools/ Industry Links Organizations are openly stating the ineffectiveness of attempting to create technological awareness at 13 +. It is in the primary school that attitudes towards the world in which we live develop, and it is in the primary school that children first become aware of the way in which they can respond to and influence that world. It is in the primary school that Design Technology can first make a contribution and here in the primary school that so many benefits are to be reaped.

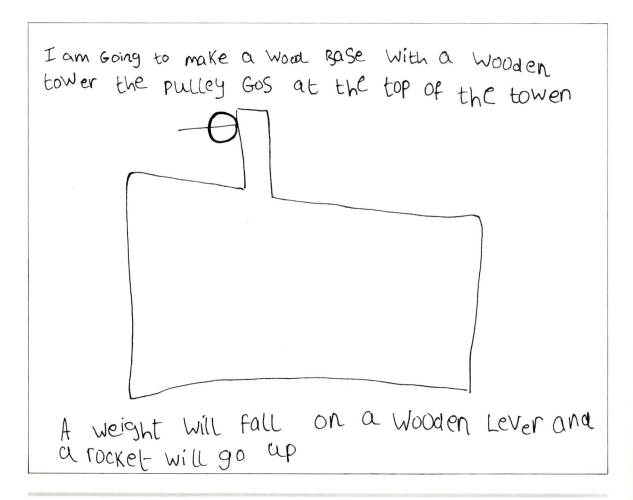

I am Going to make a Wood Base With a Wooden tower the pulley Gos at the top of the towen

A weight Will fall on a Wooden Lever and a rocket will go up

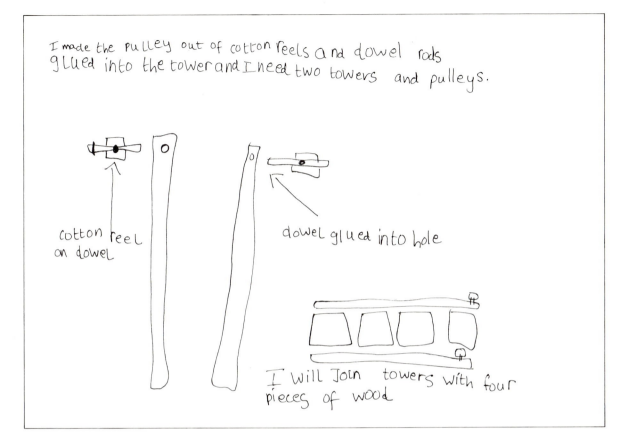

I made the pulley out of cotton reels and dowel rods glued into the tower and I need two towers and pulleys.

cotton reel on dowel

dowel glued into hole

I will join towers with four pieces of wood

to work it you have to hold the stick and shake it up and down

DISCUSSION POINTS

1   Can you identify situations in your classroom in which children *use* skills and knowledge they have acquired in a *real* situation?

2   If you are going to allow children to pursue an activity over an extended period of time what are the implications for:

> classroom organization
> school organization
> the balance of the curriculum?

4 Design Technology — What Is It?

Education must be about real things — first hand experiences. Let children look at the real world, let them touch, see, explore, smell, listen, feel — reality at a level appropriate to their development — and please, let them make decisions.

Ron Lewin and Eric Duckworth *The Need To Diverge*, TES.

All primary schools should aim to broaden children's knowledge of themselves and of the world in which they live. Through this greater knowledge should develop skills, concepts and a self-confidence which will help them to relate to other people. The most appropriate way to achieve this aim is by offering a primary curriculum that links subjects together. This has been emphasized in the Bullock and Cockcroft reports and in the Primary Survey.

Pentagonal Model

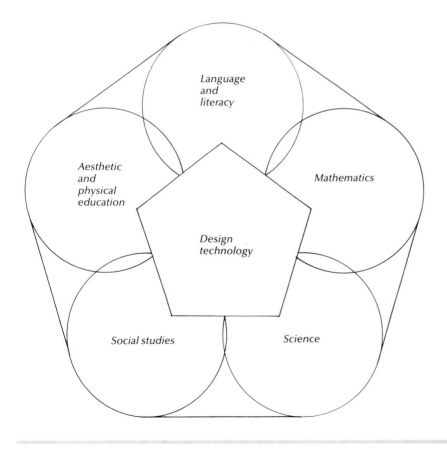

Language and literacy

Aesthetic and physical education

Mathematics

Design technology

Social studies

Science

In the pentagonal model below (Figure 1), the primary school curriculum is depicted under five broad headings: (1) Language and Literacy, (2) Mathematics, (3) Science, (4) Social Studies, (5) Aesthetic and Physical Education. At the centre of the five headings, acting as an agent for unification, is Design Technology. Design Technology in the primary school is an exciting and motivating activity. Through careful planning and sympathetic teaching, Design Technology can forge links between the classroom and the real world that exists outside the boundaries of the school. It allows girls and boys to undertake exciting journeys where changes of direction are encouraged. Children are expected to break their journey in order to 'stand and stare' and venturing into uncharted territory is openly encouraged. Design Technology can bring to girls and boys an awareness of the needs of people and society and an understanding of the world in which they live.

The ability to recognize, analyze and solve problems is now receiving recognition as an essential part of all children's intellectual development. The most appropriate point at which to start this education is in the primary phase. If what we offer children in primary schools is to be relevant to the individual's and society's needs, as we approach the twenty-first century, then Design Technology must be a part of the curriculum for all children. Children in primary schools from the age of 5+ must be given adequate opportunities to practice and develop their natural capabilities to invent, create and achieve solutions to problems relevant to the individual's stage of development. This type of creative imaginative work must surely reinforce basic skills across the whole primary curriculum.

Electricity is like water except water runs round pipes and electricity runs round wires.
Seven year-old boy, Rotherham Primary School

Primary teachers are, by the very nature of their jobs, 'Jacks-of-all trades and masters of a few', and there is no quicker way of arousing their suspicions than by presenting to them what they might construe to be the latest education bandwaggon. They need to recognize that Design Technology starts from where they are — from topics, themes and projects in which they are already involved and that it will not make more demands on what are already over-stretched financial and human resources. The majority of the work in our primary schools is based on topics, themes or projects and this is an ideal way to introduce Design Technology. Starting in the infant or first schools, we must make our children aware of technology and lay the foundations on which, hopefully, secondary and higher education will effectively build.

Technology is about solving man's material problems, but not at the expense of environmental or social considerations. Technology with a human face is the ideal balance.

E.F. Schumacher *Small is Beautiful*

Far too often we underate the ability of young children to grasp concepts which relate to real problems in the world outside school. We must encourage creative and divergent thinking from

THE DESIGN LINE

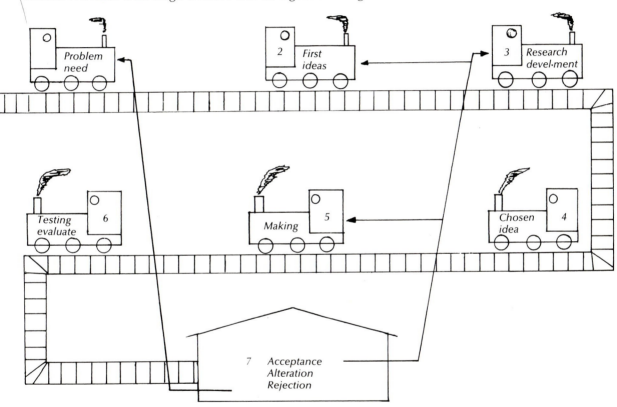

an early age. When there is a problem to solve, the 'Design Line' will help by separating the journey into a number of stages.

Obviously the problem (1) is where the process starts. This is often referred to as a need and can be relatively simple or very complicated. The problem set must be within the capabilities of the individual child or group of children. We first think of as many ideas (2) on how to solve the problem as we can, encouraging the children to be divergent in their thinking. Children will very often want to make the first idea they have, but this should be gently discouraged. There is no one correct solution to any problem and children should be encouraged to offer as many potential solutions as they are able.

The next phase requires us to carry out research (3) so that we can gather as much information as possible on which to base our selection. This will involve working with all the resource materials available in the school, at home or from any other source. This stage of our journey clarifies our thinking and results in the most appropriate of our initial ideas being selected (4). Our chosen answer to the problem then has to be made (5), using the available tools, techniques and materials. The research work carried out on stage (3) of the journey will, of necessity, include investigations into the availability of materials and tools.

When the answer to the problem has been made, then it has to be tested (6) and evaluated to establish whether our chosen design does solve the original problem. At the end of our journey (7), just as at other points along the line, it may be necessary to 'back track' to make modifications and, occasionally, we have to start all over again from the original problem. It is very rare for a solution to be perfect and in the majority of cases improvements can be made. This way of attempting to solve problems, referred to as 'The Design Line', can be applied to simple tasks set for the five-year-old in exactly the same way as it is used by much older children wrestling with what would appear to be more complicated problems. The tasks could be exactly the same, the level of sophistication would be determined by age, experience and the individual child's stage of development.

The experienced industrial engineer/designer basically uses the same process when faced by the problems that have to be solved every day. By this process the frontiers of knowledge are being constantly changed and re-written as each new challenge is accepted and worked upon to a satisfactory conclusion. Without the ability and will to solve problems then Concorde would never have flown, many diseases would not have been controlled and space travel would still be something to read about in fictional novels. The process is basically the same, whether the problem is relatively simple or extremely complex; it is the ability to cope with ever changing situations and challenges. Educating children in this way is educating them for life. Giving children in primary schools the opportunity to solve problems by making decisions helps to develop an attitude of mind that will be of immense value to them during the rest of their lives.

To broaden and enhance the education we give to our primary school children by including Design Technology in the curriculum, the individual teacher must provide a structured but flexible learning situation. Whatever the topic the children are working on, the majority of teachers, by careful thought and planning, can place the individual child, or children, in a problem-solving situation which involves girls and boys in 'thinking and doing'. Whether it be a group of six-year-olds building a space station out of cardboard boxes or, as recently in a Doncaster primary school, ten and eleven-year-old boys and girls designing and making aids to help grandparents with arthritic hands. As a result of such work they will be highly motivated by their total involvement in a decision-making process which has real meaning and relevance. Language, number, science, social skills, aesthetics — they are all included in such work. For some children it is the magic ingredient that gives them the confidence and need to talk and write about their experience.

Aids designed and made by 10/11 yr old primary children to help arthritic grandparents.

Many skills are involved in work of this kind which crosses subject boundaries and links so readily into the main areas of the primary school curriculum. Obviously problem-solving skills would be much to the fore in helping children to recognize a need and seek solutions. Craft skills would be broadened and improved as simple tools and techniques were introduced and used as and when appropriate. Various methods of communicating would be explored and improved, using words, symbols and three dimensional models. The ability to discriminate would be important when considering alternatives. General study skills would be broadened as children faced the problems of using a much wider range of resources and references with the consequential ordering and presentation of various information.

The child's ability to enquire, analyze and record would be improved as the need to research ideas and hypotheses became an important aspect of the work. The necessity to make critical judgments on individual and group activity in order that decisions can be made would be a part of the evaluation process.

Design Technology should aim to develop within the individual child a sense of values which comes from the excitement and challenge of venturing into the unknown and working through the 'Design Line' to a well-planned and well-made solution.

DISCUSSION POINTS

1   Does Design Technology fit into the curriculum in our school? Do we offer to our children an education that takes them out of school and into the real world with all its problems?

2   It is very likely that the LEA has a specialist CDT Adviser. Could he/she help in getting this type of work started?

3   Is there any industry near to the school? Could they offer our children worthwhile experiences?

But design education has a very special part to play. It is a key factor in developing practical skills and in fostering the creative and problem solving interests and talents in boys and girls. I am sure that it is important to develop these practical interests early.

Baroness Young (Minister of State, Department of Education and Science, Speech at the Design Council)

5 Design Technology — What Materials Are Needed?

If children in the primary phase of education are to be involved in 'thinking and doing' and solving problems, then they will need a range of suitable materials. The wider the choice the better, but realism is essential in terms of cost, storage facilities, the tools and techniques needed to work the materials and the skills of the teacher. Whatever boys and girls decide to make, as a result of attempting to satisfy a need, they will have to use materials. Such materials can be listed under three headings: natural, synthetic and mixed. The natural materials are those available from nature and include wood, metal, and clay. Materials that are manufactured by people are called synthetic and include glass, concrete, and plastics. The mixed group are natural materials which are altered to give them better properties: these include fabrics of various kinds — leather, plywoods and paper. As the children become more involved with a wider range of materials through Design Technology then they will decide from experience and availability which materials are most suitable for the problem they are attempting to solve.

Many suitable materials can be provided by the teacher and the children at no cost. Each day, usable items are thrown away which could be brought into school, for example cardboard boxes and tubes, plastic bottles, jars and lids, cotton reels and drink cans, old records and the lids from containers and jars. All these and many more items can be used in problem-solving work and there exists a virtually limitless supply which children and parents will deliver to school.

Other harder materials such as wood, metal and plastics will also be needed if the children are to be given the opportunity to become involved in solving real problems. However, caution is

Using "junk materials" to solve problems.

"Ramp runners" made from wood, tin lids, records and mecanno.

"Ramp runner" using Domestos bottle and tape spool wheels.

A survival shelter using thick, hard tubing.

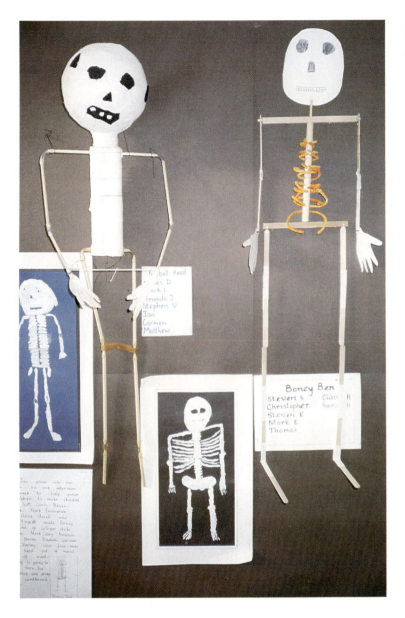

"Skellingtons" made by six-year-olds using dowel rod, clear plastic tubing and lolly sticks.

needed to ensure that materials offered for use are suitable for the intended age range. Most metals and certain plastics will pose unacceptable problems in terms of tools and techniques for both teacher and pupil, so care is essential in selecting appropriate and suitable samples. Wood is possibly the most useful of all the resistant materials and does not require sophisticated tools or techniques to achieve satisfactory results.

Lengths and sections of wood should be kept small thereby virtually eliminating storage problems, as short lengths can be kept in plastic trays or redundant crisp boxes. An excellent method of storing wood in suitable lengths is wooden tea chests which can be obtained if enough parents or local traders are asked the right question. A local builder or joinery manufacturer is an excellent source of supply for wood of all types and sizes — usually free of charge. The local education authority specialist Craft, Design and Technology adviser should be willing to assist with the conversion of the wood into sensible lengths and sections. This can very often be arranged by asking the CDT staff at the local comprehensive school for help. Some of the larger local education authorities have bulk buying consortiums for various educational materials and a primary school wood pack is very often available and sensibly priced. Such packs contain a variety of wood sections, mostly square and rectangular, but in addition have round section wood (dowelling) in a variety of diameters. Dowelling is also readily available at most DIY shops.

A selection of man-made boards should be available, in suitable sizes, for the children to examine and use. The selection would include hardboard, plywood — various thicknesses and chipboard.

Small diameter wire (metal coathangers) and copper coated welding rods would be most useful for modelling. The ease with which such materials can be cut and bent makes them ideal 'builders' for the primary school. For a modest outlay a soldering iron can be purchased and, using cored solder as the jointing medium, young children can soon acquire the skill necessary to achieve satisfactory joints. (Children must be under the direct control of a teacher when using a soldering iron).

Certain types of plastic materials can be cut and shaped using simple tools but joining these materials can become quite problematic as specialist adhesives are required which are relatively expensive and have a very limited storage life. Careful thought must be given as to whether such materials and adhesives are suitable for the primary age range. Care must be exercised in order that traditional primary school materials are not undervalued. The use of paper and card for modelling are of paramount importance, together with all the other basic materials.

It is important here to pay tribute to the excellent work being produced in primary schools using traditional materials and to stress how important these materials are. Their continued use is essential and there should be little difficulty in tying a comfortable knot between what could be termed the 'old and the new'.

DISCUSSION POINTS

1   Draw up a list of possible suppliers of suitable materials abailable at minimum cost.

2   Establish links with the local comprehensive school's CDT department. They may help with cutting materials and provide some simple tools.

3   Staff must discuss problem of storage of both materials and models. Such problems can be overcome with staff cooperation.

More emphasis than at present should be placed on work in three dimensions and some of this might be of a simple technological kind aimed at designing and making things that work.

The School Curriculum (1981)

6 What Do We Mean by Technology?

Human beings are by their very nature technological creatures: they need to know, they want to find out. Since man first appeared on this planet he has used his inborn talents and abilities to continually raise his standard of life. As problems confronted him through his development so he has attempted to solve them — some solutions were good, others were bad. He developed language in order to communicate with his neighbours, he fashioned primitive tools and weapons to build better shelters and improve his hunting capability. The problems of feeding larger numbers of people resulted in simple basic farming methods. Man has also polluted areas of his environment and caused the demise and, in some cases, the extinction of other creatures.

Only time, sophistication and scale separate these early problems from those of the present day. Technological activity varies from the relatively simple, such as the building of the model chassis or cube shown in the following chapter, to the complexities of the space shuttle.

Technology is the application of scientific, material and human resources to the solution of human needs. It can be of immense benefit to us all, but conversely it can be totally destructive. Just as modern medicine can now give a new life to people through micro-surgery and organ transplants, so technology could destroy the human race through nuclear weapons.

But technology itself is not evil. It is the way man uses it that determines its value and so it is very important that technological awareness should begin in the primary school.

There now exists in some secondary schools specialist technology teachers. This must not be the case in primary schools. Technology is inextricably linked with design and problem solving and, as Design Technology, should become an integral part of the primary curriculum. Design Technology as an integrated part of the primary school curriculum can give to girls and boys basic problem solving skills, craft skills, manipulative skills, aesthetic and technological experience at a level suitable to the child's development. The technological experience should allow primary children to look at and become involved with:

Materials: the visual, tactile and physical properties of readily available materials. How these materials can be joined, shaped and finished (colouring, polishing, etc.)

Energy: sources of energy, natural and man-made. How energy can be stored, released or transferred from one place to another.

Control: how to control devices/models that children have built. Mechanical and electrical devices to control movement.

MATERIALS

1 WOOD

There are now two main types of wood — natural and man-made. *Natural woods* are either SOFTWOODS — generally CONIFEROUS, having needle shaped leaves such as PINE or CEDAR. HARDWOODS are DECIDUOUS and have broad leaves such as ASH, BEECH or OAK. A section cut through a tree trunk would reveal the main constituent parts that are:-

Bark — the outer skin
Sapwood — the new living wood directly beneath the bark
Heartwood — this is the old dead wood in the centre of the trunk
Annual Rings — each year a new ring of wood grows directly beneath the bark.
Medullary Rays — these carry minerals and water through the trunk to feed the tree.

When trees are commercially cut down, they are converted into usable sizes as planks at the saw mill and are then SEASONED either in the open air or in a kiln.

Man-made: **Veneers** are thin sheets which are cut from logs by rotation or slicing. **Plywoods** are made by glueing veneers together with the grain of adjacent veneers being at right angles.

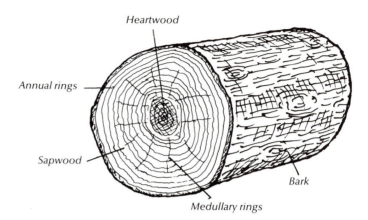

Heartwood

Annual rings

Sapwood

Bark

Medullary rings

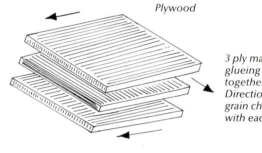

Plywood

3 ply made by glueing veneers together. Direction of grain changes with each sheet.

Blockboard

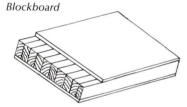

Blockboard: strips of softwood which are glued side by side and then sandwiched between outer veneers.

Chipboard: wood chips bonded together under pressure with a synthetic resin adhesive. Large flat panels can be obtained cheaply.

Hardboard: waste wood fibre is pulped and highly compressed. One surface is very smooth, the other being textured due to the manufacturing process.

2 METAL

Metals in the form of ORES are found naturally in the earth. The metal is extracted from the ore by industrial processes and can be used in a pure form or metals can be mixed together — they are then called ALLOYS. Some of the more common alloys are:

Steel — iron and carbon

Brass — copper and zinc

Bronze — copper and tin

There are two main types of metal: FERROUS which contain iron and NON-FERROUS which do not contain iron.

Great care is needed before primary children are introduced to metals, as only certain types are suitable for them to use. Aluminium is light, soft and bends easily. It is fairly cheap and readily available. Copper coated mild steel welding rods and metal coat hangers from home can be used to build interesting structures as they have the quality of giving strength with lightness. Such materials can be used in primary schools without the need of numerous expensive tools and equipment.

3 PLASTICS

When considered alongside wood and metal then plastics are a new material. There now exists a wide variety of plastics, most of which are known by their trade names, such as Perspex, Formica, Acrilan, Courtelle. They can be broadly divided into two groups: THERMOPLASTICS and THERMOSETS. Thermoplastics can be moulded when softened by heat but become solid again when cool. This process of heating, re-shaping and cooling can be repeated. Obviously thermoplastics are not used to manufacture products that need to withstand heat. Acrylic sheet (Perspex) is a thermoplastic. Thermosets become solid when subjected to heat and pressure. Once this has occurred they cannot be re-shaped or remoulded. Thermosets are used to manufacture products that must withstand heat. Most plastic kitchen utensils are made of thermoset material.

As with metals, great care is needed when selecting which plastics are suitable for primary children to use. Carefully selected and well washed plastic household containers will provide a low cost, plentiful supply of material suitable for many design technology projects. In addition to the above, Acrylic sheet (Perspex) can also be easily purchased at reasonable cost and can be bent, sawn, drilled and fastened together by adhesives. There are two types of adhesive readily available which give a high rate of success with the plastics mentioned:

1 Epoxy resin based adhesives — usually sold as two separate tubes containing resin and catalyst. These are mixed together, in equal quantities, and then applied to the surfaces being joined. Heat will usually accelerate the setting process.

2 Contact bond adhesives — well known for sticking plastic laminates (Formica) to plywood or blockwood. The adhesive is applied to both surfaces and allowed to dry before the two surfaces are brought together. These adhesives provide a very firm joint on contact.

Children should always be under the direct supervision of a teacher when using these adhesives. The adhesives should be stored, by the teacher, in a secure place.

ENERGY

Without energy our planet would be lifeless. Fortunately for us we have the sun and it is the sun which keeps providing the power for our system. Plants take energy from the sun and, in turn, they are eaten by humans and animals. Other plants, which are not eaten, eventually decay and over a period of millions of years form what we call fossil fuels: coal, oil and natural gas. These three suppliers of energy are natural resources but they are not infinite and we are now aware of the need to use wisely and conserve these irreplaceable resources.

There are other forms of natural energy. The two most effectively used by man during the development of our industrial base were water and wind. Running water in a stream or river can be used to turn water wheels. Reservoirs can store large amounts of water which can be used to produce hydro-electric power. Through the steam boiler, coal is burnt which heats water and changes it into steam, which in turn builds up pressure. By controlling how this pressurized steam is released, trains can be powered and electricity can be generated.

In the middle of the nineteenth century we had thousands of windmills in this country. They were mostly used to make flour by grinding wheat but some where used for pumping water, particularly in the Fenlands. These days there are very few left but with ever decreasing fossil fuels and rising costs we may yet see their return.

For the purpose of this book we shall briefly look at mechanical energy and electrical energy.

There are two types of mechanical energy: Potential and Kinetic. Potential can be thought of as stored energy, Kinetic is the energy of motion. If we take a child's catapult powered by an elastic band, stretch that elastic band and hold it in that position, then the catapult has Potential energy. When we release the elastic band, the stored Potential energy is changed into energy of motion as whatever object being held in the catapult is powered away — Kinetic energy. The bolt in a primed cross-bow has potential energy. When the trigger is fired and the bow string is released then the bolt has kinetic energy as it moves towards its target.

Lightning is the only natural form of electrical energy but, as yet, we are unable to control, store and consequently use it. The majority of electrical energy that we use in industry and in our homes is generated through power stations using either water, coal, oil or nuclear fuel. Batteries are the means by which we store electrical energy. There are two types with which most people are familiar. Dry batteries — those used in calculators, clocks, portable radios, and torches, and Wet batteries of the type found providing electrical power in motor cars. Batteries are devices in which chemical energy is converted into electrical energy. When a battery is not in use as a source of electricity, it must have potential energy. In primary schools we use small batteries to power small electric motors which in turn produce movement and/or control in models built by children.

Electricity: Bulbs, batteries, circuits and switches

Under no circumstances should children use the mains supply of electricity in the school. They should also be regularly warned of the dangers of using the mains supply at home for purposes of investigation. Batteries will adequately supply the amount of power required at primary level.

Many devices and machines are powered by electricity in industry and at home. The items at home are quite numerous and include such essentials as the television, music centre, washing machine, fridge/freezer. When an electric current flows, electrons move along a conductor from one point to another. The vast number of electrons moving (CURRENT) is measured in Amperes or Amps. Current flow or Amps can be measured with an Ammeter. The force in the circuit moving the electrons is called the Electromotive Force or EMF. EMF is measured in Volts and the force of the mains supply in the UK is 240 Volts. Voltage is measured with a Voltmeter.

As water moves around copper pipes, electrons usually move along copper wire which is covered with plastic or rubber. Some materials allow the electrons to move easily through them and these are called Conductors. Conversely other materials have a high Resistance to the movement of electrons and these are called Insulators. Resistance is measured in Ohms.

The units we use to measure electricity are:

Electrical current — amps
Electrical force — volts
Electrical resistance — ohms

This gives us a simple formula which providing we know any two of the three values we can work out the third. It is called OHM'S LAW:

$$\text{Electrical Current} = \frac{\text{Electrical Force}}{\text{Electrical Resistance}} \text{ or}$$

$$\text{Amperes} = \frac{\text{Volts}}{\text{Ohms}}$$

For an electrical system to work it must form a complete ring or Circuit. If the Circuit is broken at any point then the system will fail.

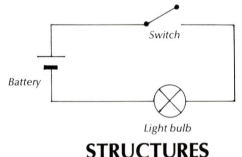

Switch

Battery

Light bulb

STRUCTURES

Structures are designed, both natural and man-made, to provide support or give stability. A structure must be able to resist forces, failure to do so will result in the structure being destroyed. To achieve structural balance, internal and external forces must match each other. External forces may be stationary (STATIC) or they may be moving (DYNAMIC). A static force is exerted on a table when an object is placed on it and remains there till the object is removed. Dynamic forces, however, are moving, such as waves or strong winds or moving vehicles (trains, lorries, cars), and they are all capable of suddenly changing in intensity. Many structural failures are caused by dynamic forces.

There are three kinds of Force: TENSION, COMPRESSION and SHEAR. When two teams are competing in a tug-of-war and are pulling in opposite directions then their rope is under TENSION. If we press an orange or lemon to extract juice, then we are using COMPRESSIVE force. A pair of scissors being used by a dressmaker to cut a piece of material are exerting a SHEARING force.

Mechanisms

There are four basic kinds of MOTION:

1 Linear — motion in a straight line in one direction.
2 Reciprocating — motion in a straight line but forwards and backwards.
3 Rotary — motion in a circle.
4 Oscillating — circular motion but forwards and backwards.

Mechanisms can be described as the parts of a machine which together create or use motion. When a machine is supplied with energy it is able to produce work. The amount of work done by the machine will not be greater than the energy supplied, indeed, in most cases it will be far less, as most machines lose energy in various ways other than doing work.

Moments

If two children sit on a see-saw and achieve balance then the see-saw is in EQUILIBRIUM. If one of the children changes their position then the see-saw will turn about its pivot or FULCRUM and this turning force is called a MOMENT. The turning moment is worked out by multiplying the force (weight of the child) by its distance from the FULCRUM (Pivot). MOMENT = FORCE × DISTANCE OF FORCE FROM FULCRUM.

Levers

A rigid beam that rotates about a fixed point is called a LEVER. We very often use LEVERS to increase the force we wish to exert. Levers are used to open large packing cases, take lids off paint tins, lift large rocks and, through a spade, to dig the garden. Levers may be categorized into three classes:

1 Where the pivot is located between the effort and load, as in a pair of pliers;
2 Where the load is situated between the effort and the pivot, as in a wheelbarrow;
3 Where the effort is applied between the pivot and the load, when using a spade to dig the garden.

Pulleys

A pulley is a wheel with a groove on its rim in which usually a rope, chain or band runs. Pulleys are used to lift heavy weights or to change the direction of motion. A car mechanic can use a pulley system to lift a heavy engine out of a car. In a single pulley system, the effort needed to lift the load is about equal (load 5 units force to lift 5 units). However, if several pulleys are used at once then the effort needed to lift the load is greatly reduced. To work out the effort needed to lift a load, count the number of ropes between the pulley blocks and divide the load by this number.

$$\text{Load} = 20 \text{ kg.} \quad \text{Number of ropes} = 4 \quad \therefore \frac{20}{4} = 5 \text{ kg.}$$

An effort of 5 kg. will be required to lift the load of 20 kg.

Gears

A gear is a wheel with teeth cut around its rim. When two gear wheels run together they are said to be in MESH. Two gear wheels running together will always turn in the opposite direction. Pulleys and gear wheels differ in that meshed gears cannot slip whereas pulleys, transmitting motion through a belt, may slip.

Pulleys and gear wheels are used to change the direction and speed of motion. If you closely examine a hand drill in a workshop or a hand whisk in the kitchen, you will see that the direction of motion is changed through 90 degrees. This is usually achieved by using 45 degree Level gears, but it could be done, in certain circumstances, by using pulleys and a flexible belt drive.

Electrical and mechanical motors usually have one speed, pulleys and gears are used to produce a range of speeds. Gears change speed by meshing together gear wheels that have different numbers of teeth. A gear wheel with twenty teeth driving a gear wheel with ten teeth results in an increase in speed. When the gear with twenty teeth turns once, the gear with ten teeth will turn twice. Conversely, a gear wheel with ten teeth driving a gear wheel with twenty teeth results in a decrease in speed. If pulleys are used to produce a range of speeds then pulleys of different diameters are employed. A large diameter pulley driving a smaller diameter pulley, through a connecting belt, will result in the smaller pulley turning faster. Conversely a small pulley driving a larger pulley will result in a decrease in speed.

DISCUSSION POINTS

1   Could a member of staff or LEA adviser organize an after-school session on basic electricity? Materials cost is moderate and the benefit for children's projects is considerable.

2   Contacts with local comprehensive schools science staff could prove positive for help with mechanisms/energy/structures. There is a considerable amount of published material available specifically for primary school needs.

3   Does the school possess any construction kits? These can be most helpful for both staff and pupils. There are many available — care is needed in selecting the most suitable for particular age groups.

The craving to design exists from a very early age if it exists at all. It can be encouraged by the right sort of environment but only hindered by traditional higher education.
Alec Issigonis,
Chief Designer, BMC.

7 Design Technology: Successful Construction

During the past five years, David Jinks has developed a simple joining technique that allows primary teachers and young children to build successfully using wood. The technique was born of necessity when, after working in a primary school, he realized the difficulties and disappointments primary children experienced when they attempted to construct with wood using traditional methods and tools.

The idea is simple and requires very little training before teacher or child can construct successfully. It consists of glueing small sections of wood together using PVA adhesive and triangles of card. Very few tools are required to build in this way, indeed, many primary schools already possess the necessary items.

Tools/materials required:

1 Junior Hacksaw: plus spare blades
2 Scissors: 12 cm
3 Rule for measuring: 30 cm (safety type preferred)
4 Pencil or marker
5 Brush or spreader for applying PVA adhesive
6 PVA adhesive
7 Small bench hook: as an aid when sawing wood
8 Card — redundant card boxes from home will do
9 Craft knife

When primary school teachers attend in-service courses designed to introduce them to this method of building with wood, they are set the task of constructing two basic models. These models have been developed to give the teachers the basic techniques required so they will feel confident in allowing the children, in their classes, to introduce the technique to their own work.

MODEL 1: THE CHASSIS

Using a word borrowed from the motor trade that described the basic frame onto which the car was built, the 'Chassis' allows children to build strong, lasting devices that will move. Basically, all that is required are four pieces of wood and twelve card triangles. The sections of wood needed are either 6 mm square, 8 mm square or 10 mm square. These sizes are the ones recommended for all constructions using this technique. The selection of the most appropriate section is determined by weight, proportion, overall appearance and availability.

The following words/diagrams/photographs show how the chassis is built step by step.

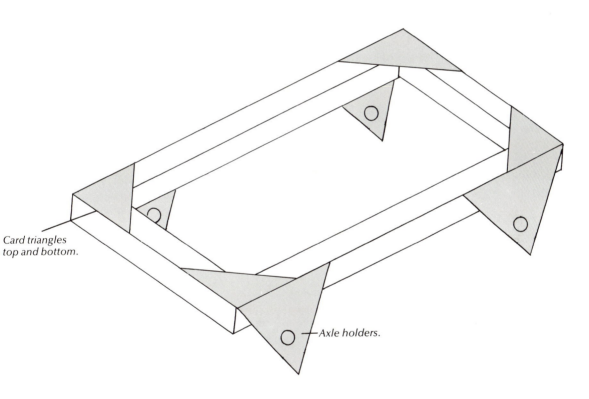

Card triangles top and bottom.

Axle holders.

1 Mark out the lengths of wood required: two at 12 cm and two at 5.5 cm

2 Cut the pieces to the required length using the junior hacksaw and bench hook.

3 Mark out eight right-angled triangles on card, each triangle measuring 2.5 cm × 2.5 cm × 3.5 cm. Cut out using scissors or craft knife and safety rule.

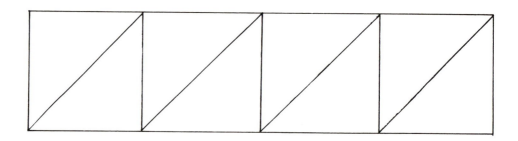

4 Apply PVA adhesive to one side of a triangle, then place the triangle onto the ends of two pieces of wood (one 12 cm and one 5.5 cm), ensuring that they are at right angles. This task is best

performed if teachers or children work in pairs, one holding the pieces of wood at right angles, the other placing the card triangles into position. The triangles should be held steady for approximately one minute to ensure initial adhesion.

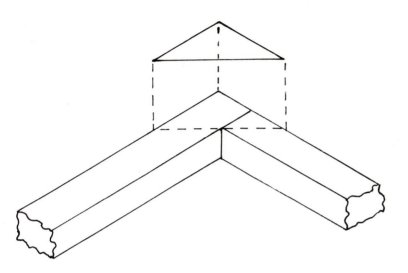

When triangles have been glued at each of the four corners then the rectangular frame is carefully turned over and the process is repeated.

5 Cut four triangles, using thicker card then previously, measuring 5 cm × 3.5 cm × 3.5 cm. These are called axle holders.

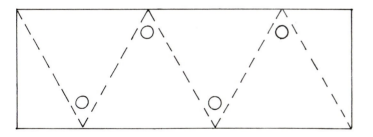

Cut accurately along the dotted lines to produce the four triangles. A hole needs to be made in each triangle where the wheel axle passes through. This can easily be done using the school's standard paper punch with the base removed. Removing the base allows each hole to be accurately located as shown in the photograph below.

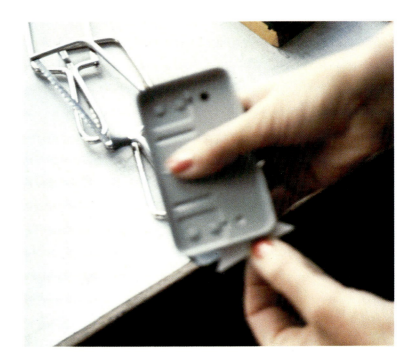

The four triangles are then fixed at each of the four corners of the chassis, using PVA adhesive, as shown in the diagram on page 61.

6 Finally, axles are located through the axle holders and wheels placed at each end of the two axles. The most appropriate wheels and axles are those contained in construction kits such as Lego, Fischer Technik, Meccano, etc., and many children will bring these to school from home. It is possible, however, particularly for older primary children for them to make their own axles and wheels. Axles are very simple to obtain by purchasing some lengths of wooden dowelling (round section) from your local DIY shop. The most useful diameter is 4.5 mm as this fits the size of hole made by a standard paper punch.

The Wheels

Building your own wheels is both rewarding and gives you the choice of making decisions about the diameter and thickness of the wheel. The process is quite straightforward and with practice will soon produce good quality wheels.

1 You need two circles of card for each wheel. The circle can be drawn using a compass which also locates the centre of the wheel.

2 Very carefully cut out the two circles — this requires patience and some skill in the use of scissors — with a little practice older primary children will soon reach a good standard. If this proves too difficult, then perfect card circles, of varying diameters, can be found in the screw-on lids of food containers (ie. coffee jars).

3 Cut a wooden lollypop stick, using a junior hacksaw, 2 mm less than the diameter of the card circle. Then, as shown in the diagrams below, glue the lollypop stick across the centre of the card circle taking care to see that the stick does not protrude beyond the outer edge of the card circle.

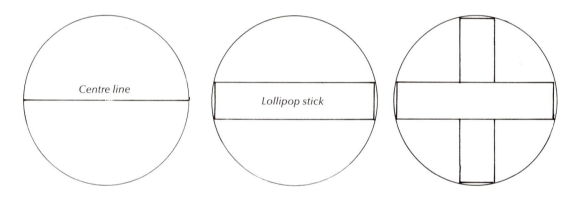

4 Cut two more pieces of lollypop stick so that they will fix at right angles to the piece already glued into position (see diagram). Again take care to ensure that the stick does not protrude beyond the outer edge of the circle.

5 Now glue the second card circle onto the stick frame, taking care to 'line up' the two card circles.

6 The wheel is now made and all that remains to be done is to drill a hole in the centre of the wheel so that the wheel can be attached to the axles. To drill the hole you will require a hand drill and a twist drill, fractionally smaller than the diameter of your axle. This ensures a tight push-on fit between wheel and axle.

Should you require wider wheels then the lollypop sticks are replaced by pieces of the square sectioned wood which will give you wheels either 6 mm, 8 mm or 10 mm in width. The photographs below show wheels of differing diameters and widths

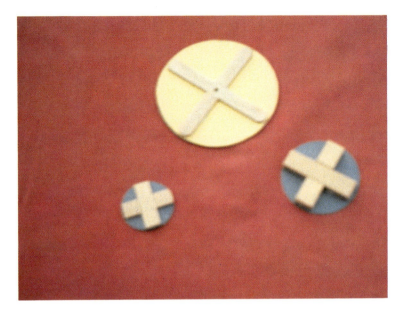

— pushed onto axles. Notice that you can cover the perimeter of the wheels with masking tape thereby producing what appears to be a solid wheel. Elastic bands or glasspaper can then be positioned as tyres to produce grip when running the models. Chassis of any size are relatively easy to build using this technique. Once the chassis is built then many types of bodies can be added constructed of paper or card to transform the chassis into a vehicle.

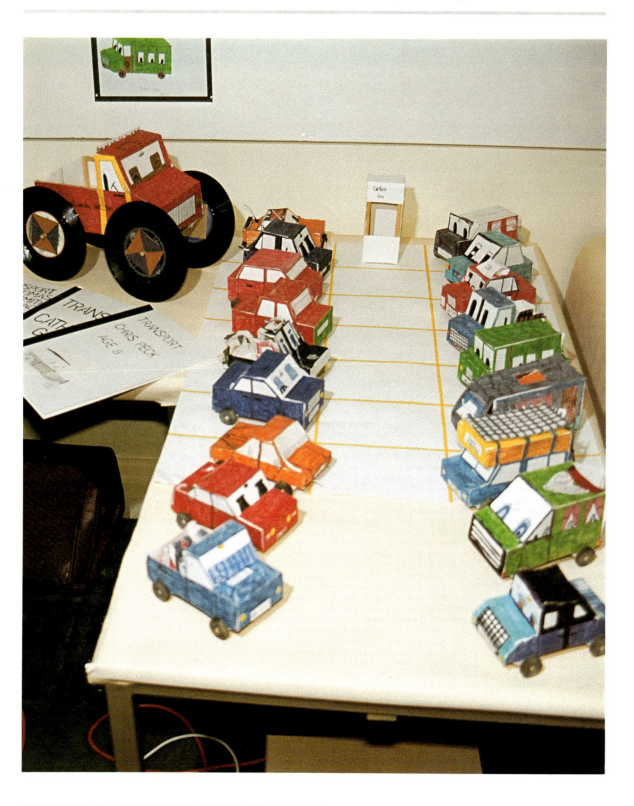

MODEL 2: THE CUBE

Just as the Chassis allows children to construct devices that have movement, the cube introduces them to the world of 'structures' (ie. bridges, houses, castles, windmills, water wheels). The tools and materials required are exactly the same as those mentioned previously for building the Chassis.

To make the cube the following materials are required:

1 Twelve pieces of wood either 6 mm square or 8 mm square or 10 mm square section

2 Eight card right angled triangles 2.5 cm × 2.5 cm × 3.5 cm

3 Eight card triangles 3.5 cm × 3.5 cm × 5 cm.

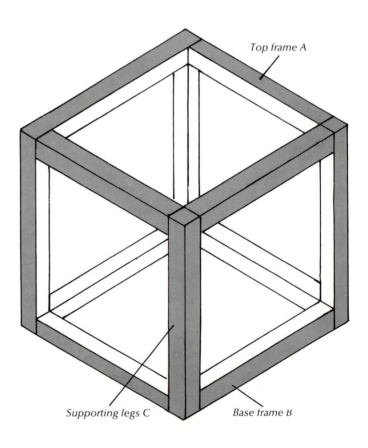

Top frame A

Supporting legs C   *Base frame B*

The cube has 10 cm sides and consists of three parts: Top Frame A, Base Frame B and the Supporting Legs C (as shown in the diagram on page 00). Using a 10 mm square sectioned wood, four pieces are required to make Frame A: two by 10 cm and two by 8 cm; the same pieces are required for Frame B. The pieces are cut using the same procedure and tools as used when cutting the wood for the chassis.

Mark out on card eight right-angled triangles exactly the same as those used for the chassis frame.

Frame A and Frame B are then fastened together using the card triangles and PVA adhesive. On the chassis frame card triangles were glued on each side of the four joints, requiring eight triangles. On the cube frames only four triangles are used on each frame.

The two frames are now made and should measure 10 cm square. Place Frame A on top of Frame B to see if they are exactly the same. The four joining legs are now cut to a length of 8 cm and these will be glued into position between Frames A and B.

To fasten the legs into position eight card triangles are needed, the same size as those used previously for the axle holders on the first model — they measure 3.5 cm × 3.5 cm × 5 cm. When the eight triangles are ready they need to be folded along their centre line and one triangle is carefully glued to each corner of Frame A and Frame B using PVA adhesive as shown in diagram.

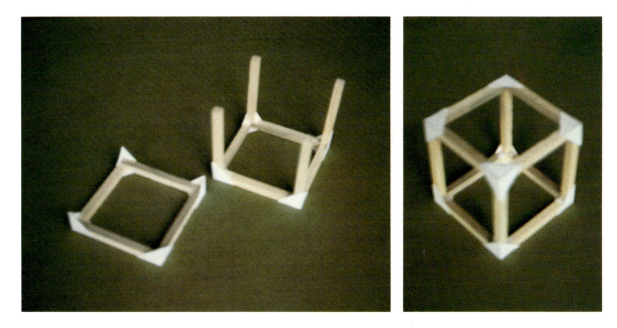

Finally, glueing the joining legs into position needs two pairs of hands in order that the process can be successfully carried out with speed and accuracy. PVA adhesive is applied to the corner triangles of Frame B and the four joining legs are placed accurately into position, being careful to keep them vertical and parallel to each other. While the legs are being positioned on Frame B, PVA is applied to the corner triangles of Frame A and this Frame is then carefully positioned on top of the joining legs. Quite often minor adjustments are needed to line up the two frames but with care these adjustments can quickly be made and the cube is completed.

On in-service courses for primary teachers building the Chassis and the Cube is referred to as 'the end of the beginning'. The simple techniques learned when building these models can be used to build virtually anything with young children. The photographs that follow show just some of the models built by primary school children and teachers using the Chassis and Cube technique. The models are strong, long-lasting and, in many cases, produced movement.

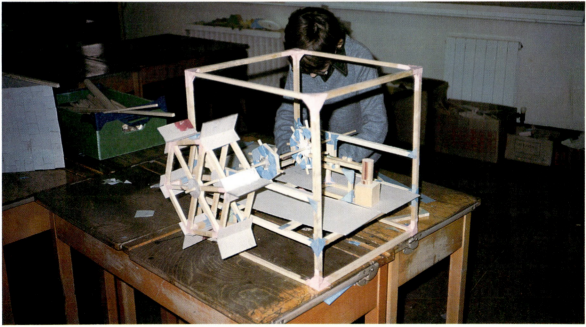

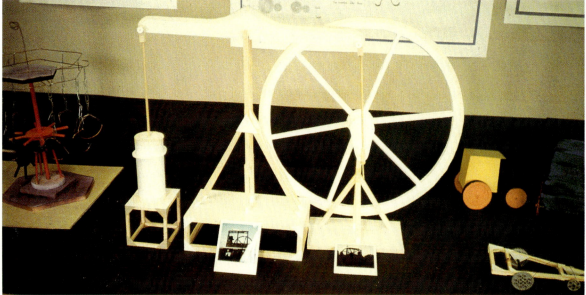

8 Communication

Our pupils, because some of them acquire skills slowly and others only with the utmost difficulty, may be in danger of spending their whole time at school in continual effort to sharpen tools which they never have opportunity enough to use.

Half our Future — The Newsom Report (1963)

The brief said 'The roller must travel a distance of 1 metre in not less than 30 seconds.' The two boys described how they had planned and constructed a zig-zag path for the roller to follow within a plywood box. 'But of course it covered the metre in under 30 seconds and so we had to look at ways of slowing it down. We lowered the angle of the paths and then the roller got stuck so we left them at the original angle and tried to increase the friction by putting patches of felt on the path. That worked alright but it took us ages to find a way of making the roller drop from one path to the other without falling off. John thought of making a guide with wire and that's what we did.' John, who had not spoken so far, pushed forward a booklet and showed a series of notes and drawings which described vividly the frustration the group had felt before they finally succeeded. The roller once more obligingly ran down the tracks. 'Not bad — that was 31 seconds' and this from someone outside the group! It was difficult not to get caught up in the enthusiasm of the group and not to be aware of how effectively they had communicated not only within the group but to the class and to us, as outsiders. The children's clear and accurate explanation, their use of precise vocabulary, and their working drawings demonstrated the ways in which the design brief had provided them with an experience with necessitated the complementary use of a variety of means of communication — oral, graphic and mathematical.

One of the interesting aspects of Design Technology is the way in which it is bringing drawing and graphical representation to the fore as a highly desirable skill for young children to develop. One of the first activities in the infant school is to draw — large brightly coloured lively pictures which are talked about to the teacher and which for the child conveys a detail and meaning which he delights in pointing out to the unaware adult. 'That's not a dog — It's a lion and he's in the jungle. He's eaten three people.' Teacher and child agree interpretation and under the pictures smaller symbols appear 'This is my lion'. But all too soon the words oust the picture — somehow it is not so important, something to be done when you've finished your work!

The Primary Survey noted 'Drawing and modelling from direct

observation was rarely encouraged' (5.87 *Primary Education in England*, 1978) and drawing was often used simply to record. Little or no mention was made of drawing as a tool, a way in which ideas could be initiated, developed and communicated. And yet it has been argued that experiences such as drawing have a vital developmental role to play for the primary age child in enabling him to develop a visual literacy, a means by which he can make a personal and individual response to the environment in which he lives. Using the experience of two-dimensional work the child develops its spatial awareness and struggles to create a picture of the world which increasingly resembles reality. In considering why art is important Eisner (1979) drew attention to the immense satisfaction the child experiences when creating images and learning that they can function also as a symbol. They learn that through creating images they can transform ideas into a public form and appreciate that some feelings can only be expressed in a visual form. There must be many children who find words difficult

Skilful planning by a 10-year-old child.

A carefully made model in balsa.

to grapple with, but who could express feeling, reason and an ability to observe accurately through their drawing. Drawing is an essential means of communication for some children and in the context of Design Technology a most acceptable way of originating and developing ideas. Far from being a frill, Eisner would argue that it has a more general role to play in the cognitive development of the child and perhaps deserves higher status as a skill than at present accorded.

In order to encourage and develop the child's ability to use drawing as a tool, it may be necessary to identify some simple skills it will be helpful for the child to acquire. Drawing a straight line, a line parallel to a straight edge, a circle, techniques of labelling — all these will increase the child's confidence in his ability to present his ideas graphically. The judicious use of broad felt pens and colour wash will heighten and dramatize the outline drawing whilst squared paper will provide guidance and accuracy which will appeal. The older junior child may find it helpful to use isometric paper as becoming aware of depth he struggles to record horizontal and vertical in a realistic way. 'Words alone are inadequate to portray the subtleties of shape, form, spatial relationships between parts, colour and texture . . . although the skills of language and number are important as they complement those of graphic communication'. (*CDT — A Curriculum State-ment 11–16 +*)

The visual response is increasingly seen by the child as having validity in the real world where comics, magazines, television, computers and advertising use a wide and sophisticated range of graphic techniques. He is aware that this is an efficient and effective method of communication and enjoys presenting his ideas in this way.

'There is an urgent need to explore new ways of working which will permit real talk'. (James Britton *Language as Educator*)

If language skills complement the graphic then in Design Technology they are given considerable reason to flourish. In planning their response to a practical problem the group of children will need to engage in a range of oral skills. In offering suggestions they will need to be able to support and justify their proposal, to question with purpose, to reason, to predict and to project. The nature of the task with its high degree of motivation encourages children to experiment with language strategies as they try to persuade others, to explain, perhaps to direct and organize. The notion of sequence becomes important as the making process is planned and carried out and causal links are established. If we take one of the uses of language identified by Joan Tough (*Talk for Teaching and Learning*) we can see how in the Design Technology situation children will be called upon to experiment with the different strategies of reporting on past and present experiences.

1 **Labelling the components of the scene**
2 **Referring to detail — size, colour**
3 **Referring to incidents**
4 **Referring to sequence of events**
5 **Making comparisons**
6 **Recognizing related aspects**
7 **Making an analysis using several features of the above**
8 **Extracting and recognizing the central meaning**
9 **Reflecting on the meaning of experiences including own feelings.**

Working together with a genuine need to communicate.

All of these strategies were present in the conversation with the group who had to fulfil the brief of making the roller. It was not enough to say it got stuck — it became necessary to use phrases like 'the end face', to explain why it fell off. One boy described his frustration after total involvement for two days and the need to get away and do something different. These were children in a village school described by their teacher as not very able or forthcoming.

Working with a range of materials and using different processes will very often necessitate a fairly complex and technical vocabulary and there is no reason why children should not be introduced to these words gradually. Some junior children were being shown around a Ready-mix concrete factory. The foreman was being helpful and carefully explaining that concrete is mixed like a cake — to a recipe. 'You mean the ratio don't you? Is that a standard mix and why do you use such a large aggregate?' The poor man was taken taken aback but rallied and quite enjoyed taking the children to the manager to discuss the 'use of retarders' in the current batch of concrete. These children had acquired their vocabulary gradually as they made and tested small concrete beams. They explained compressive strength in terms of squash and tensile strength in terms of stretch — perhaps not highly scientific but phrases which denoted a genuine understanding at their level of the concepts involved. This extending vocabulary does not just relate to one particular situation and the words will readily become part of an everyday vocabulary — thermal, plastic, brittle, malleable, etc.

In trying to extend their knowledge and clarify their ideas children will often need and wish to have recourse to books but as Southgate Booth points out in *Extending Beginning Reading:* 'Abstracting information from non-fiction texts is a complex task and the skills of paraphrasing and summarizing are notoriously difficult.' As the children use the reference library in their practical problem-solving the teacher has a genuine reason to indicate the way in which an index can be used to speed research, the need to compare reports in different books and for the older children the advantages of scanning and the ability to pinpoint the main sentence in a paragraph. 'Children cannot be expected to summarize, in writing, what they have read if they have not first been encouraged and trained to do it mentally and then express it in spoken words.' (Southgate Booth).

Working with the groups and looking at the texts the teacher has the opportunity to do precisely this. The advantage lies in the fact that it is the children who have perceived the need for the information — who need to acquire techniques of efficient research and reading, not to complete a workcard but to further a task which they consider interesting and real. The learning is taking place in a genuine context which the child appreciates as relevant.

'Children will learn to write if the writing is related to meaning-ful, purposeful activities.' (Frank Smith)

Although much of the Design Technology experience lends itself to communication through drawing, a variety of writing skills will be necessary to complement this and to ensure effective communication. It will be necessary to write concisely, isolating important facts, to label clearly, to sequence actions so that appropriate and accurate directions may be given to others. In reporting the development of the project the children can be encouraged to keep notes at each stage and then to use these at the end to produce a brief report. The group working together could produce one report which must be a consensus report — allowing them to experience the joys and frustrations of collabora-tive working. Writing in this context should be seen as part of a process, a mirroring of the real world in which inventers and designers need to inform others of their progress and achieve-ments — it is not an opportunity to say 'now write about it'!

The children at the beginning of the chapter referred to the path their roller would take. They spoke about increasing the angle of the path and had in fact worked out the gradient. In terms of the maths book they were on, they were not particularly able, but through a practical experience they were beginning to develop an awareness of the power of mathematics to communicate and explain. They would still probably have difficulty in actually measuring angles on a piece of paper but they were experiencing the practical implications of 'less than a right angle', of the relationship between distance and angle when measuring a gradient. It is this 'feel' for mathematics which Cockcroft argues is so important. The report indicated the extent to which the need to undertake even a simple piece of mathematics could induce in some people feelings of guilt and anxiety and helplessness and this was not restricted to those lacking in academic qualifications. Presenting the mathematical experience in a natural situation encourages the child to develop positive attitudes to what it sees as useful, relevant and desirable information. A small boy of six playing with cog wheels was able to make statements indicating a fairly sophisticated awareness of the mathematical concepts involved. 'The bigger wheel has more teeth than the smaller one. It goes slower than the smaller one. It only uses some of its teeth to turn the small wheel, then it uses the rest to make it go round again. They go opposite ways don't they?'

Older junior children having been given some wooden circles wanted to use them for wheels and needed to centre them. Their teacher gave them a device to do so — but why did it work and how did it work? The practical experience generates a confidence in handling such concepts because all activity is seen by the child as towards a purpose. It is not identified by the child as maths, reading or any other subject or basic skill but rather as 'something I need to know'. As adults we too learn best when we need and want to know. This is not to say that the Design Technology experience provides every opportunity necessary for all the skills and knowledge the child needs to acquire, but it does provide the observant teacher with a starting point, an opportunity for practise, a chance to evaluate genuine understanding or a point of comparison with previous learning. Because of the nature of technology it will only be through mathematics that certain aspects of the problem-solving process can be communicated as the child strives to express the complexities of numerical and spatial relationships. They will appreciate that 'it provides means of communication which is powerful, concise and unambiguous' — Cockcroft Report.

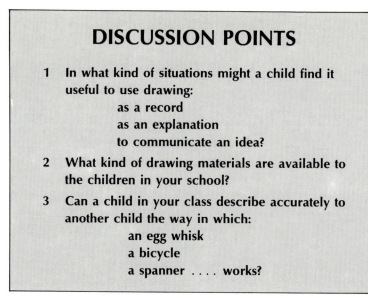

DISCUSSION POINTS

1 In what kind of situations might a child find it useful to use drawing:

  as a record

  as an explanation

  to communicate an idea?

2 What kind of drawing materials are available to the children in your school?

3 Can a child in your class describe accurately to another child the way in which:

  an egg whisk

  a bicycle

  a spanner . . . . works?

9 Case Studies

Primary schools must be declared a protected species before we destroy something that may be uniquely valuable in an educational system that daily appears to have less and less to be proud of.

Vic Kelley

'Research and the primary curriculum' *Journal of Curriculum Studies* (1981) Vol. 13, No. 3.

LEVERS AND DUCKS? 6-year-olds

Levers and Ducks? It does not seem a very likely combination does it and yet in one Infant school there seemed to be a natural and logical connection. A group of six-year-olds were being encouraged by their teacher to look at the action of a lever. She had made a simple lever using geo-strips. Carefully labelled this was displayed prominently in the classroom so that the children could reach it and see how it worked. At the same time a duckling arrived in the classroom, brought by a parent for the children's interest. The duckling was looked at, talked about, weighed, watched, listened to, had poems written in his honour and carefully drawn — in fact, well used!

The teacher showed the children an example of a lever.

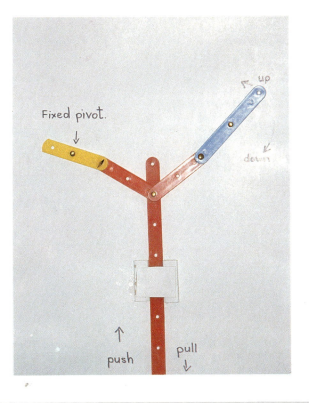

The following day after a general discussion with the class it was decided that each child should make a duckling and try to make some part of it work using levers. At this point the teacher was careful to stress and introduce specific vocabulary — lever, arm, fixed pivot, movement, etc. The children savoured these words with considerable pleasure and feelings of superiority.

Working in small groups, only one group being involved in the activity at a time, they began to try to make a duckling. A wide variety of solutions began to emerge as the children identified various areas which they wanted to move: heads, beaks, tails or eyes, all created different problems. The materials used were card and metal clips — all quite within the control of young children. Children soon identified the need for a guide if they were to be able to control and restrict the movement of their lever and these they made using glue and strips of card. They referred to the initial model made by the teacher but extended and changed it for their own purposes.

Having made a duck which they found acceptable the children were asked to draw their model and to carefully label the parts so that others would understand how it worked.

I can make my duck better

like this. I can add a
lever for the tail

open
shut

pull ↑
↓ push

my mock-up is made from card.

my levers are Geo-strips

my design for moving the beak

on my duck

This is a design to make my duck work better

I moved my big lever up and put the head onto it.

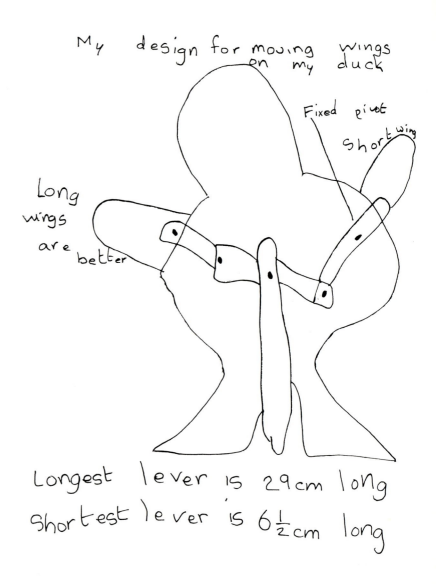

My design for moving wings on my duck

Fixed pivot

Short wing

Long wings are better

Longest lever is 29 cm long
Shortest lever is $6\frac{1}{2}$ cm long

Now they could really make their duckling. Having solved the problem of movement they could now concentrate on creating the fluffiness and appeal of the duckling.

The experience had provided the children with opportunities for very specific language development and use and an appreciation of a mechanical concept. When drawing their solution they were encouraged to identify and discuss cause and effect and to appreciate the necessity for sequencing actions when constructing any model.

Trying out the notion of the lever.

The finished moving duck.

WINDMILLS — 7-year-olds

The children in this upper infant class were working to a very particular design brief. There was to be a Technology Fair in the area and the brief was to produce a working model, powered in any way you choose but which must contain wood, plastic and metal. The model had to be accompanied by a record of writing and drawing to show how the solution had been arrived at. The children could work alone, with a partner or in a group.

The class discussed the Fair with the teacher and she asked them to draw a model they would like to make. The teacher discussed the drawings with the children. Were they practical? Could they make that? What would they use? How would they make this work? Some designs were selected for construction and work began.

The first step was to collect together the materials they would use, often just junk items, sometimes parts from construction kits in the classroom, very little was safe! Almost immediately adaptation was necessary as children found 'it didn't fit' or 'it won't work'. They identified the problem and through discussion with the group and with the teacher tried a variety of solutions. Only one group at a time made their model. One group wanted to make the sails of the windmill go faster. A direct drive wouldn't allow them to do that so why not try a chain and cog wheels like a bicycle? How big will the cog wheels have to be and does it matter how long the chain is — it keeps slipping off. Problems were encountered when the spindle revolved freely and a way had to be found to hold the spindle firm. Having overcome these difficulties the children were disappointed when the sails rubbed against the main body but found that they could make a spacer leaving the sails free to rotate.

First we collected all the stuff but when we fixed it together it didnt work

Then we changed it and put some cog wheels on it. and it only worked some times

Then we put some wooden Sails on But the Spindle turned round by it self and the Sails wont go round becase They were too long and there was a knob in the way

we put some Sand in it we put some more knobs and things on it and we made the chain smaller. And it worked better and we painted it.

The differences in the original design and the completed windmill indicate the development that took place. The ideas were there from the beginning but the process of making had allowed them to appreciate the necessity for a different drive, the effects of friction, the relationships between the speed of the sails and the size and teeth of the cog wheels. The original design envisaged cardboard sails but the group quickly appreciated the need for rigidity and looked for a more appropriate material choosing wooden strips. It is in this matching of material to purpose that young children can begin to acquire an understanding of the properties of materials and discriminate in their choice.

Neither the childrens' drawings nor their writing can convey the extent and depth of the discussion which took place within the group before a decision was made and the organizational skills exhibited as children were detailed by each other to 'go and see how that bicycle works', 'find a bigger nut' and 'write down what happened'.

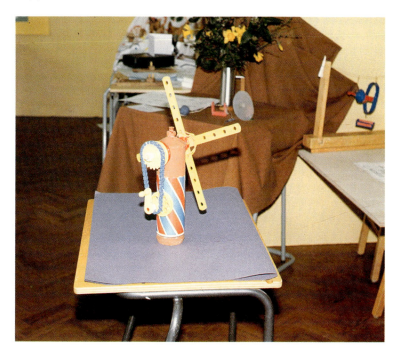

The process took time — over two days. Its justification perhaps lies in the enthusiasm with which the children demonstrated their working model and the clarity and confidence with which they explained its working and their step-by-step progress to success.

A ROMAN CHARIOT — 7-year-olds

'Infant children can't do it. Piaget says they can't!' So spoke a headteacher — responding to the suggestion that even infant children are capable of design and problem solving activities in the way we have described them. 'We'll try but what shall we do?' was the next question. The children in the school were totally immersed in 'The Romans' and so it was decided that a group would make a Roman chariot, a racing chariot, one that would move. Learning began immediately as it was soon apparent that the children had no clear idea of what a chariot was, its relative size, purpose and potential speed. Books were closely scrutinized, pictures discussed and then the children asked to draw their preliminary plan for the chariot. Together with the headteacher these plans were carefully examined.

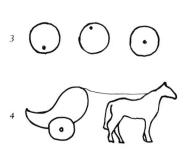

Discussion soon revealed that drawn like (1) the wheels would come off. The plan was amended (2). Perhaps this would be better but how do wheels fit onto vehicles? This necessitated a visit to the car park to examine the staff cars, and then more books and toy cars. Having discovered the axle, how do you know where to put it?

Pencils were pushed through cardboard discs and eventually the notion of centering the axle was established (3) and a further drawing produced (4).

The chariot had a very distinctive curve and the children carefully examined the marble model brought in by a parent. Making the shape could be a problem but perhaps they could find something of a similar shape. A giant size fabric conditioner bottle provided the answer, but where do we cut it? Using the marble model the children made a paper template and then put this over the plastic bottle and cut around it. Wheels were found from the junk box and the inside of a ballpoint pen provided the axle.

The children had come a long way in their problem-solving but now to attach the chariot to the horses. Cardboard horses had been made and fitted to cotton reel rollers. These were success-

The marble model provided the starting point.

The chariot made by infant children.

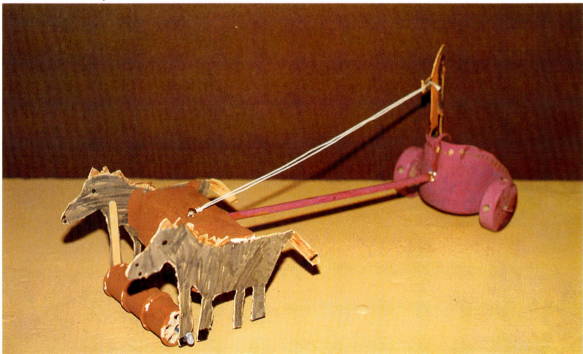

fully joined to the chariot by using a large knitting needle for the shaft, the knob holding firm inside the chariot.

The last problem remained — to make the chariot work. A rubber band was used in a variety of ways with little success until finally it was fixed to the centre of the axle and the top of the chariot — would sellotape hold? The chariot moved but discovery continued — winding the wheels backwards the chariot moved forward — guess what happened when you wound the wheel forward?

The headteacher concerned was delighted with the way the project had gone and particularly in the language opportunities it had offered and the practical maths that had ensued. The school plan to look for similar opportunities in future project work. Starting early in the school year with a small group they plan then to use these children as leaders of other groups. Infant children can do it — extremely well!

CAR DESIGN — 9/10-year-olds

Using the brief for the local Technology Fair as a starting point, the teacher had begun discussions with his class of 9/10 year olds. The brief required 'A working model — which either moves along a flat surface or is stationary and has moving parts. The energy to make the model move may be produced in any way — by hand, propeller, rubber band, electric motor, etc., and the model must be made from at least three of the following: wood, metal, plastic, wire, rubber and concrete. The children produced a vast range of ideas but by the end of the week were becoming increasingly frustrated as skill failed to keep pace with ideas — the submarine made from a plastic lemonade bottle filled with concrete to make it sink would not, under any circumstances, rise to the surface nor could its electric rudder and propeller move it under water!

To retain the challenge but to put it into a framework which both teacher and children could manage more effectively, the children were given two rectangular pieces of plywood and some cm^2 paper. They were asked to place the plywood on the paper and draw round it. In order to design the shape of their car they were to be allowed only two or three saw cuts. They must therefore experiment with the design required. They repeated this four times and from these four shapes chose the one they liked best.

Having chosen the shape they were asked to repeat the process but this time to produce four different exterior designs from which they would select the car they were to make. The shape was transferred from paper to plywood by using a pin to prick out the shape on the wood.

Initial set of 4 designs.

Design chosen with 4 different exteriors.

Because the situation was more highly structured the teacher was able to plan a process through which the children would learn specific skills of marking and cutting wood and drilling. The two pieces of wood were put together in a vice, the children using both hands on a coping saw to cut out their chosen shape. The axle holes were marked and drilled. The children now had two identical sides for their car which could be put together using nails and glue. Pieces of biro pen casing and wire coat hangers were used for spacers and axles and wheels cut by a wheel saw fitted.

At this point the experience opens up. By providing the appropriate material and taking the children through the process step by step, the teacher had ensured that thought and planning had gone into each design, that he had given each child the opportunity to use specific tools and that each child had achieved a degree of success. From this success the children felt able to capitalize on the knowledge and skill they had acquired and to seek ways to make their cars more attractive and exciting. They devised the 'Carlos Fandango' wheels using the ends of aluminium coke tins. To be sure that the wheels would match, jigs were devised to facilitate cutting out and the drilling of central holes.

Jig for making 'Carlos Fandango' wheels.

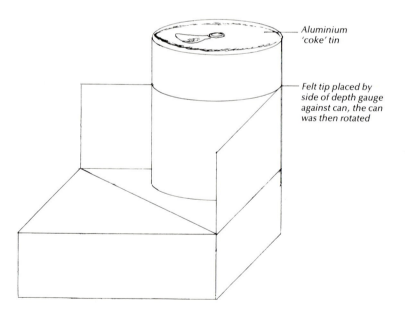

Aluminium 'coke' tin

Felt tip placed by side of depth gauge against can, the can was then rotated

Problems of friction were overcome by giving the wheels tyres of rubber bands.

It still remained to make the car move. Rubber bands were used fixed to the axle and the opposite end of the car and the differences of front and rear wheel drive explored and even four-wheel-drive. Catapults and propellers were used as were small electric motors — in the words of their teacher — 'they thought, they made, they tested'! The final results were highly diverse and ingenious but the process had allowed the children to work within constraints, to acquire specific manipulative skills and to appreciate the importance of planning and a later stage external finish. The initial success was important — it was the confidence provided by that which allowed the children to experiment at a more realistic level — but they never did get that submarine to rise!

ABBEYDALE INDUSTRIAL HAMLET
10/11-year-olds

The School has no specialist facilities for science, craft or any other practical subject and the staff — six women, two men + Head are infant/junior trained. There is, however, between the two top classes, a large non-timetabled classroom which is most suitable for practical activities and storeage. A fourth year group of girls and boys (aged 10–11) visited Abbeydale Industrial Hamlet, Sheffield, as the starting point for a project which was to last for a half term (seven weeks). The tour around the Hamlet was guided by a knowledgeable lady, gifted in the way she was able to extract information and facts from the girls and boys. The project was planned to involve all thirty-five children in Design Technology/ Problem Solving and it started, back in the classroom, with a slide/ talk/question session. The class then began work on the project from a geographical base. Abbeydale was the ideal site for such a venture because all the necessary materials, including river water, were on hand. The children then looked historically at the development of the iron and steel industry in Sheffield from these simple beginnings.

Drawings, based on careful observation, were made of the various buildings and machinery that makes up the Hamlet. Plans, to scale, were drawn of the site and considerable work was done on area and volume. Copies of an original census were obtained from the local museum service and relevant information from this was programmed into a computer data file. Information about the different working areas at the Hamlet was also stored in the computer and eventually one group of children produced a first class programme about Abbeydale Industrial Hamlet which included some excellent colour graphics.

During the seven weeks that the class worked on the project the development of number and language skills was carefully monitored. The improvement in social interaction within the class was particularly noticed by the class teacher and headteacher.

The variety of work undertaken by the children as a result of the initial visit, studying the slides, and exploring the many excellent books on all aspects of the topic soon generated a sequence of practical work. All the children in the class were fascinated by the water wheels they had seen and very quickly were constructing their own simple working models. Some children improvised a method of construction using discarded household containers such as custard powder containers or syrup tins. This initial practical work which came so naturally from study in other curriculum areas soon led into work on other forms of energy and power.

One group of boys decided they would like to build a large working model of the TILT FORGE complete with a water wheel that would power the Tilt Hammers that were to be housed in the

Forge building. A group of girls sketched out their designs for the GRINDING HULL, again to be powered by a water wheel. Other boys and girls became involved with wind power and large working windmills were designed and constructed. The

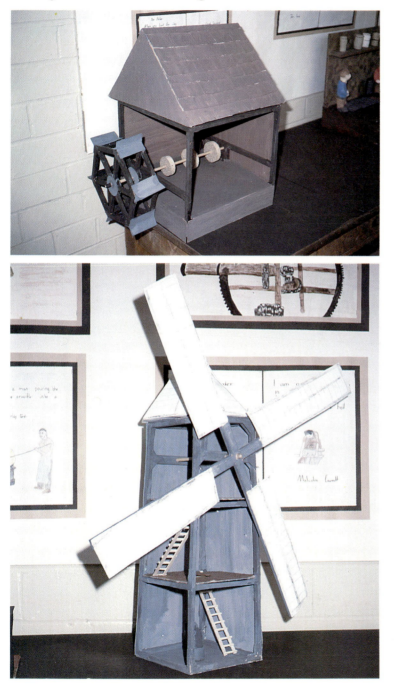

MANAGER'S HOUSE was built out of card, wood and clay, complete with acrylic windows and opening doors (lollypop sticks). The working end of the CRUCIBLE FURNACE room was realistically modelled by some girls — they included in their model two furnace workers and scaled down clay crucible pots with lids.

The use of tools went hand-in-hand with the use of books from the resource area. Many children brought information from home including old photographs and articles from newspapers/magazines. Everywhere in the classroom was evidence of meaningful integration between the 'practical' and the 'academic'.

Boys and girls talked about changing the direction of movement, the problems of friction, power/weight ratios, and sketches were used to reinforce verbal explanations. The development of language skills in thinking, talking and writing was very obvious, as were the graphics based on careful observation. The practical problem solving work was a natural part of the primary school day and there was no conflict between time spent on developing numeracy and literacy and that given to the practical aspect of the project.

Resources of various types are of great importance when children are asked to work in a 'thinking and doing' way. Slides and pictures together with information sheets and charts, reference books of all types — particularly with pictures for certain children — are essential in providing information and reinforcement. The class teacher had provided a basic selection of books on 'Water Wheels' and these, and other topic areas, could easily be supplemented by books from the library/museum service.

The work displayed around the school itself constituted a learning source. The class teacher had taken care in mounting a classroom display that undoubtedly stimulated ideas for work on the Abbeydale topic. People are excellent 'resources' for primary children and should be fully utilized. The caretaker at the school was so impressed with what he saw the children doing that he became involved in the topic. He talked to the children about his work when he was employed in the local steel industry and this led eventually to him building, alongside the children, a working model of a drop forge hammer.

The high standard of work produced by the children in this class across the primary curriculum was undoubtedly due to the professional commitment of the class teacher. Her careful planning and sympathetic teaching guided the boys and girls on an exciting journey which travelled along many different roads — with adequate opportunity to stand and stare — and occasionally venture into unmarked territory.

The tools, techniques and materials used to enable the children to be successful in their practical work were inexpensive and did not require elaborate in-service work to enable the class teacher to feel confident in guiding her children. This is evident in the way the same tools, techniques and materials are now being used by other teachers in the school, so that their children can also experience the joy of making things that work and last.

CONTROL TECHNOLOGY
PROBLEM SOLVING: 11/12-year-olds

The school, originally designated infant/junior, became a first/middle in 1979. This involved employing one extra teacher giving a total staff of one Head plus seven teachers. Minor alterations were also made to the building in 1980 to create a 'science area' and provide storage cupboards and work surfaces in the 'wet areas' between each pair of classrooms in the middle section of the building.

The teacher responsible for science decided to work with a class of thirty 11/12 year old boys and girls on Control Technology/Problem Solving, attempting to link the practical problem solving work to the BBC micro computer.

The boys and girls in the class were allowed to choose a topic to study and eventually formed four groups of approximately equal numbers. The chosen topics were (i) Security systems; (ii) Conservation of energy; (iii) Traffic control on land, rail and water; and (iv) The weather. Investigations took place into the four topic headings from the resource material provided within the school and from external sources. Very commendable work was achieved by these children in what can only be described as a very demanding project for both children and teacher.

The boys and girls looking at house security systems began their research in ancient times and discovered many fascinating locking devices. Children in the group made locking devices from wood, and one boy designed a lock built entirely out of Lego which was operated by an electric motor. The group eventually built a large model of a house which had the usual number of windows and doors. These were all fitted with reed switches and magnets which were then interfaced to the computer so that when any particular window or door was opened then the appropriate information would be shown on the monitor screen.

The group working on the conservation of energy were able to obtain masses of information on this subject from a variety of sources, including government departments. Sifting through all their material they became interested in the problem of heat loss and the necessity for adequate insulation. Experiments ranged from how to keep a cup of hot liquid at maximum temperature for as long as possible, to the study of the performance of different insulation materials for wall cavities and roof areas. This work

resulted in a model house being constructed which had cavity walls and a large roof area. These areas were insulated, in turn, with a wide range of materials and probes, situated at appropriate

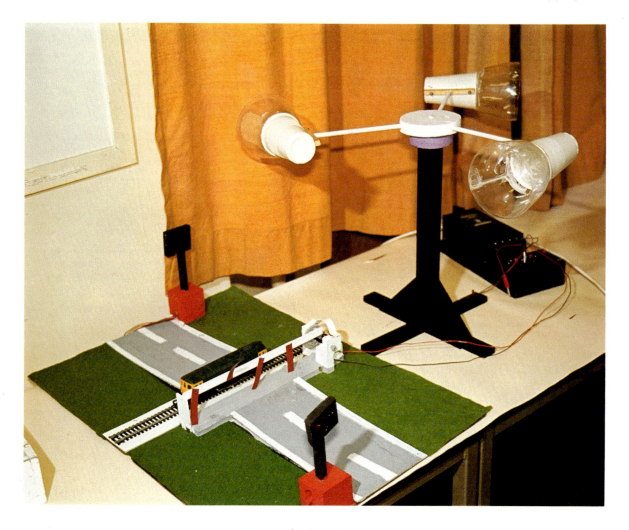

points and relayed information back to the BBC computer which recorded temperature fluctuation over a pre-determined period of time.

The children working on traffic control looked at traffic on rail, road and water. This work involved them in building a level-crossing model of considerable size which had flashing red lights to indicate to the road transport that the way was unsafe, and a computer-activated barrier system to prevent vehicles crossing the line when a train approached. Another group tackled the problem of controlling road traffic across a river, and a bridge was designed that could be raised and lowered on a series of pulleys, again activated by the computer and again using a system of

flashing lights to warn the road vehicles that the bridge was raised, allowing free passage to the water bound transport.

Two boys looked at controlling traffic on canals and devised a very ingenious way of moving water from one level to another using a series of levers which facilitated the movement of the water. This did not involve any work with the computer but finished as a delightful model by the two boys after a considerable amount of hard work.

This school had recorded daily weather conditions for many years so it was appropriate that 'the weather' would be a part of the top class children's problem solving/computer project. The computer was used as a data base to store all the records built up over many years. Children designed and built devices that would record through the computer, the direction and speed of the wind. Experiments were conducted into the monitoring of both internal and external temperatures.

The very commendable work achieved by the children in this class across the curriculum was due to the enthusiasm and commitment displayed by both the pupils and the teacher.

10 Kits

Technology becomes understandable through experience

Fischer Technik — *School Programme*

This is not, as you might expect, a quotation from an educational journal but the heading on an advertizing leaflet for a particular construction kit. Going into any school it is difficult not be aware of the continually increasing range of construction kits which are now available. The brightly coloured plastic has pushed aside the large wooden bricks and the kits are seen not just at infant level but through the primary school and into the secondary stage. Seeing the children happily engaged with the variously shaped pieces, it makes sense to ask how these activities fit into the overall curriculum and the way in which the experiences provided through the construction kits will extend children's learning.

The kits are very varied, presenting a variety of sizes and shapes of building blocks which link together in differing ways. These are accompanied by more specific accessories such as wheels, play people, trees, car bodies, signs, gears, caterpillar tracks and axles. The building blocks vary in size from the large Lego Duplo to the smaller precise building systems of Fischer Technik. It is clear from the accessories that the manufacturers are aware of the need to provide kits which will enable children to extend and refine their early conceptual development. The present rash of kits offering opportunities to experiment with mechanical and electronic functions indicates their awareness of the current educational thinking that even sophisticated concepts can be presented in a simple way, given the right materials, and that children want and are able to take their models closer to reality.

Attitudes to the use of construction kits vary considerably. In the Nursery they are widely used as a play experience. The opportunity they create for effective group interaction is widely appreciated but not often is the material used in any structured way to develop notions of shape, form, colour, etc. Many infant teachers see the play with construction materials as a useful stimulus for language activities but this is only effective if the adult interventions are planned and well timed. Frequently 'playing with Lego' is the reward for finishing 'work' — something done in the afternoon perhaps whilst the teacher hears children read. We have heard lower junior teachers explain a few children playing on the carpet with 'They are rather young for their age and so I let them play with the Lego some afternoons'. Obviously this is not always the case but what is disturbing is the feeling that these systems are in some sense not 'work' and of less importance than reading or number. We no longer question the value of material or matching games in developing number concepts and pre-reading skills so perhaps we need to consider that there are many scientific and technological concepts which can more readily be developed through the practical manipulation and construction of apparatus than any number of formal lessons. Surprisingly too, even at infant level, construction materials are implicitly assumed to be of more interest to boys than girls.

What emerges is that few schools have any clear idea of the way in which these construction kits can contribute to children's learning and for this reason are often choosing materials which are inappropriate or make demands which the child is not able to respond to. An element of over expectation exists in which the child presented with the brightly coloured materials will immediately respond and will be able, almost instinctively, to use these materials. There will be a fairly immediate play response but to extend the experience requires consideration of the demands the material makes and of the problems the children may encounter. The blocks fit together in differing ways. The kits offer a variety of tools and fixings such as screws, nails, nuts and bolts and push-fit systems. Do we leave the child free? Free to what? Discover how it works? True if that is the objective but if we expect the child to complete a particular task perhaps it is necessary to draw his attention to the way the fixing works or the appropriate tool so that then he can concentrate on the task in hand. Many kits contain workcards for the child to follow. These make considerable assumptions about the child's ability to interpret certain graphical conventions. Even the apparently simple card which shows:

1 All the parts necessary to make the object
2 A stage by stage guide to construction
3 A photograph of the completed model

assumes many skills. The child needs to be able to match colour, size and shape and to also accept the two-dimensional stylized representation of the three-dimensional object. They must then appreciate the notion of sequencing actions, perhaps lines used to indicate motion or a perspective drawing. For some infant children this is too difficult and they need a long period of play with the material, talking with the teacher about the parts before

they can attempt to use the cards. Within the same class there may well be groups of children not only capable of following the graphic instructions but also capable of following more sophisticated conventions such as those of an exploded diagram. This is not really surprising if you think of the spread of reading ability we experience in many classes. Having completed the construction, discussion often remains at the descriptive level and children are not encouraged to identify the causal relationships they have established or the particular properties of the structure or mechanism. In this sense an under expectation exists as opportunities are missed for clarifying and drawing out much of the learning implicit in the activity.

To ensure that the most appropriate materials are chosen and that children derive full benefit from their use we need to be clear about the ways in which they can be used to extend, vary and enhance learning opportunities. As a play experience they can help the young child to sort, match and establish concepts of

Some infant children can handle very sophisticated digrams. These children used the exploded diagram to construct their model.

Using the kit material to explore an idea.

shape, colour, form and movement. They will help to develop imagination and creativity and provide opportunities for role play and decision making. At a later stage they are used to help construct graphs, explain fractions, create sets and measure areas.

Using these materials the child can begin to establish an understanding of a wide range of concepts — balance, suspension, gearing, hydraulics, faces, steering, drive, etc. What we are anxious to ensure is that a progression in understanding is achieved.

> **Although all children progress at varying rates they do tend to follow specific patterns. For example:**
> — **from simple to more complex and complicated activities and skills.**
> — **from unplanned and experimental to structured activities.**
> — **from concrete to abstract ideas and concepts.**
> *The Lego Educational Programme*

Attention has already been drawn to the way in which the materials lend themselves for language development as parts are named, colours and shapes identified and creations discussed and explained. Many of the kits are designed for group use and there is therefore the further possibility of language extension in a natural group discussion context. Using these materials makes demands on the manipulative skills of the child and also develops hand/eye coordination. This may be particularly important for girls.

It is common knowledge that lack of early activities involving spatial awareness and insufficient experience with mechanical toys and puzzles are important contributory factors to the later unachievement of girls in mathematics and science.
We Can Do It Now (Equal Opportunities Commission.)

Playing with constructiion material is an essential stage as children learn the properties of the material.

Perhaps the most important use of kits at the junior level will be to allow the child to model and to express ideas. The child who says 'How do I know what I think until I hear myself speak' may also need to see his ideas working to appreciate a difficulty or a development. Used in this way construction kits are not presenting ready-made solutions but enabling the child to represent ideas to himself and to others and to see the results of action, the interrelationship of parts, through physical means.

Whatever material is used 'appropriate' is again the key word. We need to consider whether it will be used by a group or individuals, for demonstration or explanation or as an aid to specific problem solving situations. As the child matures this appreciation of technology increases and he seeks to achieve greater reality in his models. The materials he works with must facilitate this and we are fortunate now in the choice of materials we have.

Knowing why we use construction kits and what we expect from them, we are in a position to support children in their play and discovery, to provide what direct instruction is necessary and to ensure that they have the skills and language necessary to let 'technology become understandable through experience'.

DISCUSSION POINTS

1   Are construction kits available to all the children in your school?

2   What specific vocabulary can you identify which the children will require in using these kits?

3. What assumptions are made by the workcards or other graphic material with the kit?

It is the quality of the pupils united experience of designing, planning, making, testing and evaluating that is of fundamental importance rather than any ability he or she may acquire in a specific competency. Designing and making should be central activities in CDT... it is through these activities that CDT makes an important contribution to the preparation of boys and girls for adult life in a changing technological society.

CDT — A Curriculum Statement for the 11–16+ (1983)

11 Planning a Curriculum for Design Technology

Although written to refer to older children the quotation applies equally well to the primary child. **CDT** is an approach to learning that does not base itself on subject divisions but it is still possible to describe the kinds of experiences we wish children to have, the learning outcomes we hope for the children, and the organization necessary to allow this to take place.

Schools are being strongly urged on all sides to identify, clarify and evaluate the curriculum they offer.

> **The curriculum needs to be viewed as a whole and to take account of different needs and abilities, to be concerned not only with what is to be learned but also how it is to be learned.**
> *The School Curriculum (1981)*

and again:

> **This thinking will surely be more productive if teachers have a clear idea of what they are trying to achieve and how they will know whether they have been successful.**
> *The Practical Curriculum (1981)*

We have already spoken of the diffidence with which many primary teachers approach Design Technology activities. It is essential that a teacher knows and understands exactly what a school is trying to achieve. The curriculum policy must ensure continuity and progression, it must be specific enough to support the hesitant or inexperienced teacher, and yet it must be open enough to allow each teacher to bring their own interests and enthusiasm to bear and to exploit opportunities as they arise so that the learning fits into an overall context. This may seem a daunting and lengthy task but a simple strategy can help them to achieve a concise curriculum statement.

FORMULATING A POLICY FOR DESIGN TECHNOLOGY

A policy is intention on the part of the staff to identify knowledge skills and attitudes and plan an organizational framework which will allow children in the school to:

(i)   identify real problems
(ii)   examine possible/alternate solutions
(iii) decide on an optimum solution
(iv)   plan a sequence of working
(v)   carry out the task to a required standard
(vi)   evaluate the total process
— in the context of Craft, Design Technology.

STAGE 1	**As a staff discuss and decide on what you mean by Design Technology.**

The following definition may help or you may wish to use films such as *Technology Starts Here* DES (Central Film Library) and to start your discussion.

Craft, Design and Technology is essentially a practical problem-solving process which involves the whole being, physical, intellectual and spiritual. As a process it involves and provides purpose for other studies and, because it is concerned with real things, it provides a recognizable context for a variety of learning and thinking to take place. The practical nature of the activity creates an involvement in which disciplines are seen in context, immediate feedback increased understanding of their limitations, evaluation is essential and acceptable, and within which confidence and competence can grow. Against this background it is possible to develop a range of skills, as children working in groups learn to co-operate, to compromise, to plan and construct, to make decisions and through the excitement and pleasure of creation to encourage self fulfilment and a positive appreciation of the value of doing.

Curriculum Guidelines for CDT (Berkshire 1984)

> **STAGE 2** | **Discuss the reasons for doing Design Technology in your school. Consider these aims and objectives or you may wish to write your own.**

Aims

(i) To develop an awareness of the environment and to appreciate that we can affect and control this environment.

(ii) To develop the child's ability to communicate effectively — verbally, numerically and visually.

(iii) To appreciate the variety and nature of materials and the ways in which they may be worked.

(iv) Through the creative use of materials to develop initiative and a range of thinking and practical problem solving skills.

Objectives

For us to be able to plan at classroom and school level we need to translate these aims into a series of objectives for which we can plan and resource so that children will be offered appropriate experiences. For a primary school such a set of objectives might be:

(i) Through a range of materials to provide children with a sensory experience of a visual and tactile nature.

(ii) Through critical observation to encourage children to observe, identify and understand elements of design in the natural and man-made world.

(iii) To bring together information and knowledge from many areas and to use this information in a practical problem solving situation.

(iv) To appreciate the particular qualities of common materials.

(v) To provide a variety of constructional activities which will encourage an understanding of simple technological principles.

(vi) To appreciate the safe and appropriate use of certain tools and develop skill in their use.

(vii) To identify and accept drawing as a useful tool for expressing, communicating and developing ideas and to provide simple skills for this purpose.

(viii) To develop cooperative, leadership and organizational skills.

(ix) To make reasoned judgments following methodical enquiry.

(x) To permit children to experience a sense of satisfaction and achievement in directing their own learning.

STAGE 3 | **It is necessary now to identify exactly what concepts, skills and attitudes you wish to establish.**

It may be helpful to consider skills and attitudes under various headings:

Skills
(i) Practical
(ii) Communication
(iii) Reasoning

Attitudes
(i) to oneself
(ii) to others
(iii) to the environment.

From 5–13 it is more helpful to concentrate on a limited number of concepts, in particular those concerned with:

Materials
Energy
Structures
Control

For each of these concepts it is possible to formulate a series of statements which will help to define it. You are then able to plan appropriate activities and experiences which will allow children to develop an awareness and understanding of this concept.

Materials
1 Different materials possess different physical and aesthetic qualities.
2 The properties of a material determine its use.
3 The properties of a material determine the tools necessary to work it.

Using the matrix which follows, activities have been suggested at three stages. Detailed planning such as this gives teachers confidence in developing design technology and makes it easier to resource the activities well.

Statements describing the concepts	Infant	Lower Junior	Upper Junior
1 Different materials possess different physical and aesthetic qualities	(i) Simple sorting hard/soft, strong/weak, stretch/non-stretch. (ii) Classification (iii) Collection and identification etc.	Extend sorting vocabulary and range of materials. Classify according to sensory response: feel — smell	(i) Collect materials with particular properties — tensile strength, malleability (ii) Consider one resistant material in detail — origin — manufacture — use — properties
2 The properties of a material determine its use.	(i) Classification and consideration. Materials used for clothes for houses for furniture (ii) Make a kite) „ „ boat) „ „ weight) and analyze materials used etc.	Take one material and identify its properties. Find as many instances as possible of its use. Classify these instances according to properties.	Design and make a toy — carefully list needs — materials and properties and then choice.
3 The properties of a material determine the tools necessary to work it.	Match-scissors to .. -hammer to . . . -saw to . . . etc.	Match cutting tools — how many — what are they used for?	(i) Consider the tools used to work one material. How was this worked historically? (ii) Make a tool to work a particular material.

You will also need to consider concepts such as Energy, Structures and Control and these are clearly and simply stated in Chapter 6 and 'An introduction to CDT in the Primary Curriculum' produced by Coventry LEA.

Energy

Energy is the capacity to carry out work, for example to pull or push an object. Energy can be produced and 'stored' in a variety of ways:

 as fuel — coal, liquid gas, food, etc.

 as electricity — battery.

 mechanically — clockwork motor.

 — rubber bands (twisted or stretched)

 compressed air ⎫
 ⎬ subject to safety considerations
 steam ⎭

Energy can also be drawn from 'natural sources' such as wind, water or sunlight.

Energy can be changed from one form to another. When 'stored' as a fuel or as water in a reservoir it is 'potential' energy. When converted into movement (for example petrol or steam engine or electric motor) it becomes 'kinetic' energy. It can also be turned into light or heat forms.

Structures

Certain concepts listed under 'Materials' also promote an awareness of structures. However, specific attention should be paid to the following:

(i)   the load a structure can carry is not directly linked to the amount ('thickness') of material used;

(ii) the 'strength' of a structure depends upon the way in which its parts are arranged and joined — for example an electricity pylon;

(iii) triangular shapes are basically 'stiff';

(iv) rectangular shapes are 'flexible' unless braced — (ii) above;

(v)   a structure is stable when its 'weight' stays over its base, even when rocked.

Control

(i)   the transmission of energy or its conversion from one form to another can be controlled in a variety of ways. Mechanical control can be brought about by using cranks, cams, levers, gears or pulleys. Electrical/electronic control can be brought about by using manual switches, electrically operated switches, sound or light sensitive switches;

(ii) the application and control of technology in everyday life carries serious social implications.

If similar grids are completed for skills and attitudes a concise policy is produced which has the merit of allowing the teacher considerable freedom. The lower junior child considering the properties of materials may do this as part of a project on'Myself', 'Our House', 'The Senses', or under many other guises. What is essential is that he is learning to discriminate between materials and extending his vocabulary to enable him to express this difference.

Stage 4	**The organizational factors which will facilitate the policy.**

Getting Started

Whilst the ultimate aim is to have this work arise naturally from what is going on in the classroom, a school beginning to develop its design technology activities may decide to structure them more tightly at first as children and staff explore the approach together. This can be done by setting a particular design brief for the class or classes: 'Put a matchbox on the table. Can you make something which will move it to the next table? You may not touch the matchbox with your hands.'

The brief is very open, not restricting the children at all in their solution or the materials which will be used. If the whole class is involved it will be more easily managed if they work in groups. Parents can help a great deal too as the children need to talk through their problems and solutions with a supportive adult as well as with each other. The purpose of the exercise is two fold — to solve the problem of course, but also to provide the children with a kind of workshop training so that they are sure how to handle and use tools, where they may be used and where and how they are stored. It is also important that they realize you expect the process to take an appreciable amount of time and are willing to allow this. From the beginning it is necessary to stress the need for planning — not just the design but which materials are to be used and how they are to be cut, fixed, shaped and finished. Encourage the children to sketch as they go along and to keep these sketches as a way of communicating the kind of thinking which took place in their solution.

Having set the brief it should be possible to anticipate some of the questions — not all — that the children will ask and to have books on display and easily available. There is no need for their problem-solving to start from scratch and for them to struggle reinventing the wheel. Using other people's ideas as a basis is an acceptable problem solving strategy.

It might be helpful to devise the design brief in two parts so that all the class produce its first part and are left free to plan the second. Perhaps making a simple car, even using a template, the emphasis being on developing specific practical skills and routines: sawing, drilling, marking, shaping etc. The second stage will be to make the car travel 1 metre and stop. The success of the first stage is important for teachers and children alike!

Stage 5	**The Resource Implication of Design Technology**

Human Resources
Will you involve parents? What will their role be? Will you give them any guidance before they work with a group?
As a staff, have you anyone with Design Technology experience? Would your local secondary school design department help you by running a practical session with simple tools in their workshop for your staff?

Materials
What materials will you use?
Wood, plastic, metal, wire, card, concrete, rubber?
Where and how will these be stored?
Are there small items you will need to purchase — propellers, motors, wheels, pulleys, etc.?
What books in your library will support design technology?

Tools
Are the tools you have appropriate (i) in size (ii) in kind?
Are the tools in good condition?
Are they easily available to the children?
Have you established procedures for their use
(i) with children
(ii) as a staff?

Time
What arrangements might prevent children having uninterrupted periods of time?
Will these be suspended or will the activity have to be stopped and restarted?
How will you plan to allow children the time they need?

Space
Where will children store models under construction?
How will you organize the space in your classroom?
Is there a safety advantage in having tools used in one area of the classroom only?

As a school you should now have established what Design Technology means for you, how it will take place in your school and what you feel it will offer to your children. Like all plans, however, the policy will eventually have to be reviewed.

Stage 6 | **Evaluate and Review**

(i)   Has Design Technology contributed to the children's development in any of these areas:

Confidence	Cooperation	Language skills
Ingenuity	Leadership	Mathematical skills
Practical Skills	Planning ability	Hand/eye coordination
Reasoning ability	Manual dexterity	
Organization	Motivation	

(ii) What new learning opportunities have your children been offered?

(iii) Is there a progression of experience for children through the school?

(iv) Does Design Technology have in-service implications for your staff?

(v)   What particular problems have children/staff encountered?

(vi) Do you need to reconsider your resources?

> to replace/renew
> to buy new items
> their position and storage
> maintenance
> appropriateness
> distribution around the school

12 Starting Points

1 Make something which will travel across a table top and stop at the edge.

2 Devise something which will allow you to stand a metre away from a table and turn a page in a book without touching it with your hands.

3 Make a model which has two different movements.

4 Using only one A4 sheet of thin card/paper support the heaviest weight you can at a height of 10 cms.

5 Make a conveyor belt.

6 Construct something which will travel in circles.

7 Use weight to create movement.

8 Make a pump.

9 Devise a machine which will measure out equal amounts of sand/water.

10 Make something which will travel backwards and forwards along the same line.

11 Lift an object from floor to table.

12 Lower an object from table to floor.

13 Construct a timing device which rings a bell after 30 seconds.

14 Devize an interesting journey for a marble.

13 Useful Addresses

E. J. Arnold & Sons Ltd.,
Parkside Lane,
Dewsbury Road,
Leeds LS11 5TD

Suppliers of a wide range of educational equipment.

Association for Science Education,
College Lane,
Hatfield AL10 9AA

Numerous publications on science and technology.

British Federation of Sand and Land Yachts,
181 Highbury Road East,
Lytham St. Annes,
Lancs.

Interesting topic for primary children.

British Gas Education Service,
326 High Holborn,
London WC2R 7PT

Brochure available giving details of publications and AVA on aspects of energy and on gas supplies.

British Petroleum Educational Service,
P.O. Box 5,
Wetherby,
West Yorks, LS23 7EH

Free catalogue listing booklets and AVA material on Children and Energy and a Series on Plastics.

British Steel Coporation,
Information Office,
12 Addiscombe Road,
Croydon, Surrey

'Iron Ore' leaflet/poster   50p
'Making Iron' leaflet/poster 50p
'Making Steel' booklet   80p

Buck and Hickman Ltd.,
P.O. Box 33,
23–32 Whittall Street,
Birmingham 4.

Wide range of tools and ancillary equipment.

R. S. Components Ltd.,
P.O. Box 472,
13–17 Epworth Street,
London E.C.2 P2HA

Wide range of electrical components.

Cement & Concrete Association
Conf. & Training Centre,
Fulmer Grange,
Slough SL2 4QS

'This is Concrete' — booklet and work cards
'Concrete Toadstools' — booklet
'The History of Concrete' — booklet

The Conservation Trust,
246 London Road,
Earley,
Reading RG6 1AJ

Numerous study notes for teachers on such topics as: Trees, Transport, Energy, Alternative Technology — all 25p each.

Department of Energy,
Thames House South,
Millbank,
London SW1P 4QJ

A comprehensive primary school pack on Energy.

Electricity Council,
30 Millbank,
London SW1P 4RD

'Understanding Electricity' gives comprehensive details of free material on Electricity/Energy.

Esso Petroleum Co.,
Education Services,
Public Affairs Dept.,
Victoria St.,
London SW1E 5JW

Good range of wallcharts and booklets on energy. Send for most recent catalogue.

Fitchett & Woollacott Ltd.,
Willow Road,
Lenton Lane,
Nottingham NG7 2PR

Timber merchants to schools for many years.

Frank Gadsby Ltd.,
High Street,
Lincoln.

Daler board and specialist card.

Glass Manufacturers Federation,
19 Portland Place,
London W1N 4BH

Various leaflets about glass, its history and uses.
'Bottles and Jars' a project book — 5p

Griffin & George Ltd.,
285 Ealing Road,
Wembley,
Middlesex HA1 1HJ

Suppliers of a wide range of educational equipment.

I.C.I. Ltd.,
Schools Liaison Officer,
Millbank,
London SW1P 4QG

A wide range of useful publications — send for most recent list.

Kodak Ltd.,
P.O. Box 66,
Hemel Hempstead,
Herts HP1 1JU

A wide variety of Kodak publications and AVA which can be used in education at all levels. Contact the Customer Relations Dept.

Letraset Ltd.,
St. Georges House,
195/203 Waterloo Road,
London S.E.1

The catalogue, if available, is very useful.

PEL Ltd.,
P.O. Box 15,
Rood End Road,
Olbery, Warley,
West Midlands, B69 4HN

Educational furniture of all types. Plastic storage trays.

Porter (Selby) Ltd.,
Station Road,
Selby,
Yorkshire, YOB 6NP

The timber merchant produces Primary/Middle school Timber Packs, at reasonable prices, which contain sensible sizes of wood. These packs can be delivered — discounts for orders of 20 packs and over. Contact for details.

Record Ridgway Tools Ltd.,
Education Service,
Parkway Works,
Sheffield S9 3BL

Suppliers of tools — literature and posters.

Reed Group Paper Division,
Educational Service,
New Kythe House,
Aylesford,
Maidstone.

Information sheets on paper — its history — how to re-cycle. Charts on paper making.

Ripmax Ltd.,
39 Parkway,
London N.W.1

Gears and electric motors.

Science & Technology Regional Organisations (SATROS)
The National Liaison Officer,
SCSST,
1 Birdcage Walk,
London S.W.1H 9JJ

Write and ask if they provide help and support in your area for primary science and technology.

Shell U.K. Ltd.,
Shell Education Service,
Shell-Mex House, Strand,
London WC2R 0DX

Good range of material available — send for most recent catalogue.

Stanley Tools Ltd.,
Woodside,
Sheffield S3 9PD

Range of publications and wall charts available from their educational service.

Strand Glass,
Brentway Trading Estate,
Brentford,
Middlesex.

Suppliers of plastics materials in small quantities.

Surplus Buying Agency,
Woodbourn School,
Woodbourn Road,
Sheffield S9 3LQ
Tel. 0742 — 448647

Wide range of good quality surplus materials at cheap prices. Send S.A.E. for current stock list. Official County/School orders are accepted.

Timber Research & Development Association,
Hughenden Valley,
High Wycombe,
Bucks, HP14 4ND

A selection of information sheets and wall charts on timber.

Trylon Ltd.,
Thrift St., Woollaston,
Wellingborough,
Northants.

Suppliers of plastics materials in small quantities.

Welding Rods Ltd.,
Mansfield Road,
Aston,
Sheffield S31 OBS
Tel. 0742 — 872401

Suppliers of copper coated mild steel welding rods — 1.6 mm diameter.

K. R. Whiston,
New Mills,
Stockport,
Cheshire

Send for catalogue — wide range of fastening devices, materials, adhesives etc. A good selection of short length (13") materials.

BIBLIOGRAPHY

Coventry Lea (1983) *An Introduction to CDT in the Primary Curriculum*, Coventry LEA.

Department of Education and Science (1978) *Primary Education in England*, London, HMSO.

Department of Education and Science (1981a) *CDT — A Curriculum Statement — 11–16 +*, London, HMSO.

Department of Education and Science (1981b) *The School Curriculum*, London, HMSO.

Department of Education and Science (1982) *Education 5–9*, London, HMSO.

Duckworth, E and Lewin, R (1981) 'The need to diverge', *Times Educational Supplement*, 22 May.

Eisner, E (1979) 'The contribution of painting to children's cognitive development', *Journal of Curriculum Studies*.

Equal Opportunities Commission *Equal Opportunities in CDT*, Equal Opportunities Commission.

Equal Opportunities Commission *We Can Do It Now*, Equal Opportunities Commission.

Girls into Science and Engineering (1978) *Initial Survey*, London, Hodder and Stoughton.

Keith-Lucas Report (1980) *Design Education at Secondary Level*, London, Design Council.

McGough, R (1969) *Penguin Modern Poets 10*, Harmondsworth, Penguin.

Schools Council (1981) *The Practical Curriculum*, London, Methuen.

Schumacher, EF (1975) *Small is Beautiful*, Abacus.

Shaw, DM and Reeve, J M *Design Education for the Middle Years*

Smith, F (1982) *Writing and the Writer*, London, Heinemann.

Southgate-Booth, V. (1981) *Extending Beginning Reading*, London, Heinemann.

Tough, J (1979) *Talk for Teaching and Learning,*, London, Ward Lock Educational.